NOMOS
GLASHÜTTE

In support of

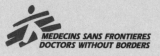

MEDECINS SANS FRONTIERES
DOCTORS WITHOUT BORDERS

Time for life—with limited edition timepieces in support of Doctors Without Borders/ Médecins Sans Frontières. Each watch raises 100 USD, GBP, or EUR for the Nobel Peace Prize winning humanitarian organization. And still these handcrafted mechanical watches with the red 12 cost the same as the classic models from NOMOS Glashütte. Help now, wear forever.

Funds raised are donated to Médecins Sans Frontières USA, UK, or Germany, depending on the specific model purchased. For MSF UK, the registered charity no. is 1026588. Available at selected retailers in the three participating countries, as well as online. Find your nearest NOMOS retailer at **nomos-glashuette.com** or order online at **nomos-store.com**.

GRANTA

12 Addison Avenue, London W11 4QR | email editorial@granta.com
To subscribe go to granta.com, or call 020 8955 7011 (free phone 0500 004 033)
in the United Kingdom, 845-267-3031 (toll-free 866-438-6150) in the United States

ISSUE 138: WINTER 2017

PUBLISHER AND EDITOR	Sigrid Rausing
DEPUTY EDITOR	Rosalind Porter
POETRY EDITOR	Rachael Allen
ONLINE EDITOR	Luke Neima
ASSISTANT EDITOR	Francisco Vilhena
DESIGNER	Daniela Silva
EDITORIAL ASSISTANTS	Eleanor Chandler, Josie Mitchell
SUBSCRIPTIONS	David Robinson
UK PUBLICITY	Pru Rowlandson
US PUBLICITY	Elizabeth Shreve, Suzanne Williams
TO ADVERTISE CONTACT	Kate Rochester, katerochester@granta.com
FINANCE	Morgan Graver
SALES AND MARKETING	Iain Chapple, Katie Hayward
IT MANAGER	Mark Williams
PRODUCTION ASSOCIATE	Sarah Wasley
PROOFS	Katherine Fry, Jessica Kelly, Lesley Levene, Jess Porter, Vimbai Shire
CONTRIBUTING EDITORS	Daniel Alarcón, Anne Carson, Mohsin Hamid, Isabel Hilton, Michael Hofmann, A.M. Homes, Janet Malcolm, Adam Nicolson, Edmund White

This selection copyright © 2017 Granta Publications.

Granta, ISSN 173231, is published four times a year by Granta Publications, 12 Addison Avenue, London W11 4QR, United Kingdom.

The US annual subscription price is $48. Airfreight and mailing in the USA by agent named Air Business Ltd, c/o Worldnet-Shipping USA Inc., 156–15 146th Avenue, 2nd Floor, Jamaica, NY 11434, USA. Periodicals postage paid at Jamaica, NY 11431.

US Postmaster: Send address changes to *Granta*, Air Business Ltd, c/o Worldnet-Shipping USA Inc., 156–15 146th Avenue, 2nd Floor, Jamaica, NY 11434, USA.

Subscription records are maintained at *Granta*, c/o Abacus e-Media, Chancery Exchange, 10 Furnival Street, London EC4A 1YH.

Air Business Ltd is acting as our mailing agent.

Granta is printed and bound in Italy by Legoprint. This magazine is printed on paper that fulfils the criteria for 'Paper for permanent document' according to ISO 9706 and the American Library Standard ANSI/NIZO Z39.48-1992 and has been certified by the Forest Stewardship Council (FSC). *Granta* is indexed in the American Humanities Index.

ISBN 978-1-909-889-03-3

English National Ballet

BAUSCH
FORSYTHE
VAN MANEN

AN ELECTRIFYING TRIPLE BILL

Tanztheater Wuppertal Pina Bausch performing *Le Sacre du Printemps*. Photo by Uili Weiss © Pina Bausch Foundation

SADLERSWELLS

Sadler's Wells Theatre
sadlerswells.com
020 7863 8000

🔵 Angel

23 MAR – 1 APR 2017

ballet.org.uk

A co-production between
English National Ballet and Pina Bausch
Foundation in collaboration with
Tanztheater Wuppertal Pina Bausch.

LOTTERY FUNDED
ARTS COUNCIL ENGLAND

Registered Charity 214006

National Theatre

'Quite probably the greatest theatre on the planet.'

Time Out

Twelfth Night

Tamsin Greig is a transformed Malvolia in this new production.

Travelex £15

UGLY LIES THE BONE

Award-winning American playwright Lindsey Ferrentino makes her UK debut.

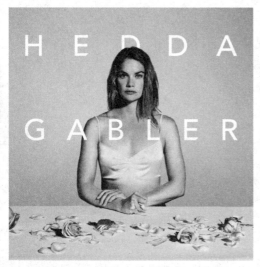

HEDDA GABLER

A new version of Henrik Ibsen's classic by Patrick Marber, featuring Ruth Wilson.

CONSENT

Nina Raine's powerful new play puts justice in the dock. A co-production with Out of Joint.

Playing this spring
South Bank, London SE1

Twelfth Night photography (Tamsin Greig) by Frederike Helwig, *Ugly Lies the Bone* photography by Mads Perch, *Hedda Gabler* photography (Ruth Wilson) by Léa Nielsen, *Consent* image: Lovers (6) © Jarek Puczel.

Travelex £15 Tickets Sponsored by

travelex.co.uk

The Dorfman Partner

neptune
The Real World Investors

Supported using public funding by ARTS COUNCIL ENGLAND

INTERVIEWS   NEW WRITING

PODCASTS   VIDEOS

...FROM AROUND THE WORLD

litshowcase.org

International
Literature
Showcase

PRAIRIESCHOONER

BOOK *prize series*

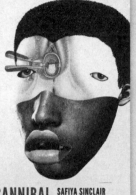

2015
Winners

PRIZES
$3,000 and publication through the University of Nebraska Press for one book of short fiction and one book of poetry.

ELIGIBILITY
The Prairie Schooner Book Prize Series welcomes manuscripts from all writers, including non-U.S. citizens writing in English, and those who have previously published volumes of short fiction and poetry. No past or present paid employee of *Prairie Schooner* or the University of Nebraska Press or current faculty or students at the University of Nebraska will be eligible for the prizes.

JUDGING
Semi-finalists will be chosen by members of the Prairie Schooner Book Prize Series National Advisory Board. Final manuscripts will be chosen by the Editor-in-Chief, **Kwame Dawes**.

HOW TO SEND
We accept electronic submissions as well as hard copy submissions.

WHEN TO SEND
Submissions will be accepted between **January 15** and **March 15, 2017**.

For submission guidelines or to submit online, visit prairieschooner.unl.edu.

EWAN FERNIE

SHAKESPEARE FOR FREEDOM

WHY THE PLAYS MATTER

"invigorating and original, powerful and thoughtful."

Peter Holland, University of Notre Dame

Publishing Spring 2017
cambridge.org/shakespeare4freedom

Your First Step to Korean Literature

SUBSCRIBE FREE today at koreanliteraturenow.com and enjoy the best Korean fiction, poetry, interviews, book reviews, essays, and more.

Korean Literature Now is an excellent publication, beautifully produced and full of fascinating articles. It is a must-read for anyone interested in Korean Literature, and literature in translation more widely.
- Max Porter, Granta Books

Korean Literature Now gives us the news about Korean writers and their works, this generation, the now gen, as well as the longer-established yet no less notable Korean authors whose works inspire and challenge us.
- David McCann, Harvard University

With its beautiful new design inside and out, excellent color images, and careful editing, *Korean Literature Now* is an invaluable gift of contemporary Korean writing to worldwide readers.
- Frank Stewart, *MĀNOA: A Pacific Journal of International Writing*

CONTENTS

Introduction

Two authors recently accused *Granta* of colonial high-handedness. One complaint was trivial; the other, about a proposed photoessay, less so. But whether the accusations were valid or not, they did make us think about the state of travel writing now.

Granta has long been associated with this particular form of creative non-fiction. It was sometimes more creative than readers and editors knew, as in the case of Ryszard Kapuściński, the Polish journalist and travel writer best known for his reportage from Africa in the 1960s and 1970s. Artur Domosławski's 2010 biography revealed that many of Kapuściński's most vivid vignettes, like the story of Haile Selassie's lapdog Lulu peeing on the shoes of visitors, courtier ready with a satin cloth, were inventions. 'Ryszard Kapuściński – the hero of Ryszard Kapuściński's books – is also a fictional character,' Domosławski memorably wrote.

Bruce Chatwin, too, has been criticised for being cavalier with facts. Like Raymond Carver, Chatwin explained nothing – you fall into his travel stories, and stay there. Are they true? Maybe. Not the whole truth, perhaps, but who can ever tell the whole truth? He captured atmospheres – that was enough, then. Editors now set more exacting standards for their writers. Fact-checking is easier with the Internet, of course, but there is also a nervousness about what you can publish and write. Public shaming is easier too, and bland generalities multiply in the mainstream while fringe publications and right-wing radio shows revel in provocations.

And sticking to the truth, of course, is not the whole story. Travel writing is about place, but it is also usually, one way or another, about people, the inhabitants of those places to which the author travels. These people are, by definition, different from the author, and can be exoticised, objectified or mocked in any number of ways. But I still think that writing about other people doesn't have to be an exercise of power or a theft of identity. It can be done with engagement, empathy and respect.

I also wonder if, in fact, any writing is innocent of objectification or misrepresentation. Every piece of text is a story, and every story has a point of view, with its own preconceived notions, potentially harmful (or beneficial) to others.

But of course this kind of cultural relativism is on the wane. I am writing in New York – it's late November and Aleppo is falling, but the news here is dominated by Donald Trump's tweets. The commentators are flummoxed. They hardly know how to talk about a president-elect who is so openly disdainful of the complex presidential web of constitutional principles and historical conventions. Mr Trump seems determined to show that he is a regular guy – an ordinary insomniac, incensed by this and that, prejudiced and angry and not afraid to show it. Post-truth, and post-shame.

The expression 'going after' has spread like a virus since this awful election campaign. Mrs Clinton used the phrase repeatedly, I guess to show that she was tough; Mr Trump hardly needed to say it, he just did it. Now everyone in the political arena and beyond is *going after* this or that.

I am here to judge *Granta*'s next Best of Young American Novelists issue (Spring 2017) with our jury of writers, A.M. Homes, Ben Marcus, Kelly Link and Patrick deWitt. The American Civil Liberties Union has kindly lent us office space and we are in a lovely boardroom, spacious and pleasantly gloomy, surrounded by books. The restrooms have signs to say that you can use the facility of the gender you identify with – a sign of the times, and yet it also feels like an artefact of another era. Trump's election is a kind of revolution. How will we talk about it, I wonder, in time? ∎

Sigrid Rausing

from *Borderland*, 2009

BETWEEN GREAT FIRES

William Atkins

The wall is an army in brown. It is fabricated in sections ten girders wide, eighteen feet tall and crowned with a metre-high blade. To watch the slatted world on the other side, Mexico, as you walk through the city of Nogales, is to be reminded of a zoetrope's flickering image; the same sequence played again and again. The steel, untreated, is red-brown with rust, and this rust in turn has leached into the wall's concrete base and drained down its sides to the ground.

The wall divides the town – Nogales Arizona/Nogales Sonora – though most of the population lives on the Mexican side. On one of the slopes on the US side is a shrine. Ranged along a reinforcement joist slanting from the wall's concrete base are some burnt-out tealights in glass jars. Knotted to the vertical palings above are a length of curled yellow ribbon and, tied in place with the same kind of ribbon, a bunch of dirty plastic daisies turned brittle by the sun. Nogales Sonora, on the other side, is twenty feet below, and I realise that the wall stands on its own embankment – steep on the Mexico side, like a castle dyke. In order to climb the wall from Nogales Sonora you first have to climb the slope. About thirty-eight feet, all told. Through the wall, in Mexico, I can make out a white, windowless building and a sign: DESPACHO JURIDICO, legal office. Stencil-sprayed on the adjoining wall, a young man's face – a boy's really, in its chubbiness – repeated over and over, like a crude Warhol, like a picture of a martyr.

José Antonio Elena Rodríguez died in Mexico; the bullets that killed him were fired here in the United States. It happened on an October night in 2012. Border Patrol had been called to a report of men climbing the wall. As the agents converged, the men climbed back over to Nogales Sonora. A crowd gathered on the Mexican side and began throwing rocks, over the fence, at the patrolmen. Among the rock-throwers was José Antonio Elena Rodríguez (this is the official version). José Antonio Elena Rodríguez threw no rocks, he was merely walking past the fence on the way home from basketball (the unofficial version, the version told by Rodríguez's friends and family and other civilian witnesses on the Mexican side). The Department of Homeland Security has declined to release its video footage of the incident. It would compromise national security. Everyone agrees that José Antonio Elena Rodríguez was sixteen.

On the twenty-foot-high bluff, behind the eighteen-foot-high fence, stood the eight Border Patrol agents. Among them was Lonnie Swartz. At the foot of the bluff was José Antonio Elena Rodríguez, walking home from basketball, or throwing rocks – both, perhaps – throwing rocks over the top of the fence, thirty-eight feet above him. Again there is no question that Lonnie Swartz approached the fence, and drew his pistol, and shot down on José Antonio Elena Rodríguez, hitting him ten times from behind, pausing only to reload.

The federal investigation rested not only on whether Swartz's actions were reasonable – he feared for his life, went the defence, rocks big as pomegranates raining down – but whether the killing could even be described as criminal when the kid was a Mexican in Mexico, and therefore exempt from the protections of the US Constitution, and his killer an American in America.

A man stands on an alluvial fan below the Tumacácoris, a few dozen miles north of here. His name is José, too: José Salazar Ylarregui. This is 1851. He is a senior member of the Joint United States and Mexican Boundary Commission, responsible for surveying the newly defined southern border. Until 1851 there was no line, no wall. It was war that created the line, the Mexican–American War of 1846, or rather the Treaty of Guadalupe Hidalgo that was the war's culmination. Salazar, jointly responsible for some hundred men, in the unspeakable heat of the Sonoran Desert, on constant guard against Apaches, made a note. Maybe he imagined his superiors in their cool Mexico City drawing rooms: 'On paper one easily draws a line with a ruler and pencil.'

In the east, that line followed the natural barrier of the Rio Grande River; in the west it travelled, originally, from El Paso along the Gila River to its confluence with the Colorado, and thence in a straight line to San Diego Bay, placing much of today's southern Arizona in Mexico. The Gadsden Purchase of 1853 caused the western portion of the line to be repositioned further north. From then on the border, rather than following the course of the Gila, was a straight line from El Paso to the Colorado. Upon a stretch of desert where there were few natural features, and fewer names on the maps of either nation, significance was conjured.

The nature of the border did not escape those tasked with making it a reality. One member of the 1851 survey, observing the newly designated borderlands, asked simply: 'Is this the land we have purchased, and are to survey and keep at such cost? As far as the eye can reach stretches one unbroken waste, barren, wild, worthless.' Another described a 'sterile waste, utterly worthless for any purpose than to constitute a barrier'. Travelling in the region in 1909, the Norwegian explorer Carl Sofus Lumholtz wrote that 'the sensation was that of walking between great fires'. Until the twentieth century the border was little more than notional: a line on paper echoed by a string of obelisks on the ground, each one separated from its neighbours by two miles of desert; further where conditions were harshest. The statesman's desert, from the Chinese Taklamakan to the Libyan Sahara: a bulwark, a buffer. But more than that, a weapon for turning your enemies to dust.

S ince the 1990s a doctrine known as 'prevention through deterrence' has been practised by Border Patrol. Even today, only 351 miles of the 1,954-mile border are effectively fenced – 18 per cent. Increasingly, Border Patrol is deploying remote electronic surveillance technology, the so-called 'virtual wall' – infrared cameras, motion-sensors, radar, drones, blimps – but in many places you can still pass from the southern side to the northern with a single step, even if that step must be flanked by a hundred thousand others. Eight kilometres east of Nogales, where the Santa Cruz River crosses (or is crossed by) the border, the fence simply stops, and all one need do in order to move from one country to another is edge along the river's bank.

The militarisation of the borderlands was accelerated following the terrorist attacks of 2001 and the creation of the Department of Homeland Security. By obliging those who are determined to cross illegally in the harshest areas – the Organ Pipe Cactus National Monument west of Nogales, say – the strategy became one whose efficiency can be measured not only by the number of would-be migrants discouraged from embarking (which is anybody's guess), but by the number of human remains recovered from arroyos and the shadows of ironwood trees. Between October 2000 and September 2014, in southern Arizona alone, this number was 2,721. Among these people – who succumbed to heatstroke or dehydration, or fell from cliffs or died of snakebite or heart attacks – some eight hundred are unidentified. To this number may be added those remains that have *not* been found, either because of their remoteness or, more likely, because they have simply been erased.

Like most deserts, the Sonoran is walled in by mountains: to the north and east are the Colorado Plateau, the Rockies and the Sierra Madre; to the west the Sierra Nevada. It is the Sierra Nevada that is responsible for much of south-west America's aridity, removing the moisture from the Pacific's clouds as they are drawn up its western flank. They call it a rain shadow, but the effect is not so much a shadowing as a milking. It is from the low-lying south – the tropical south of central America – that the monsoon comes, and the result is a desert that, while being dry enough to kill dozens of people each year, can feel deceptively abundant.

Sometimes the desert preserves – 2,000-year-old mummies have been found under the sands of the Taklamakan, their tongues still pink – but more often, it obliterates. Those shapes helixing high above, shuddering on their huge wings, are turkey vultures, and with the coyotes and the foxes they will strip a body of meat and disperse its bones over a square mile in the course of a few days. As you wait on the Mexican side of the border before trying to enter the desert, therefore, you do so in the knowledge that it is not just your life that you are staking, but – in the absence of your corpse or, if your corpse is recovered, any way of identifying it – your loved ones' opportunity to grieve for you.

After 9/11, the Department of Homeland Security evolved a new method of 'deterrence'. It was called 'enforcement with consequences'. Until then, those apprehended in the desert were processed and dispatched to the nearest port of entry without prolonged detention. This was called 'voluntary departure', because the migrant waived his or her right to a judicial hearing. Naturally, once removed from the country, they attempted to cross again as soon as possible – the next day, why not, since they'd come this far. 'They know the game,' said a patrolman interviewed at the time. 'They're delayed eight hours and then they do it over again.'

Part of 'enforcement with consequences', since 2005, is Operation Streamline. It is here that the element of deterrence comes in. Instead of being allowed to leave the US under the terms of 'voluntary departure', apprehended migrants are instead processed through the federal criminal justice system. Under Operation Streamline, first-time offenders can be sentenced to up to six months in jail, repeat offenders up to two years.

The city of Tucson lies some sixty miles from the Mexico border, and is often the first objective of undocumented migrants trying to cross the Sonoran Desert. It is also where those who are picked up by

Border Patrol are taken for trial. Given the vast numbers of people – tens of thousands – apprehended each year, it is not possible for due process to be applied. This is the nature of streamlining, and it is visible if you go to Tucson's federal courthouse on any weekday afternoon.

'Please rise,' says the judge.

A massed jangling as sixty young men get to their feet. They are manacled and fettered. It is an old, old sound, this jangling, not new to the USA or anywhere else. It is nauseating.

'When your name is called, please rise and say, *present*.' They are tired, and slow. They have come, most of them, directly from a cell, having been picked up in the desert in the past twenty-four hours. Who knows how far they have walked or how long it is since they slept? They look around. The courtroom is cool, high-ceilinged and bright, its walls lined with pastel-coloured fabric. How strange to find yourself here: those days trudging over the hills and arroyos, your clothes shredded by cacti, the birds circling overhead; and then to be transported first to a cell and then to this hushed theatre with its air of privilege, itself symbolic of what you have been seeking, and your appointed attorney placing his bejewelled hand on your shoulder.

'Jesus Manuel García,' reads the judge.

'*Presente.*'

They are called up to stand before the bench in groups of five or six, the same formulation repeated again and again.

'Mr Manuel García, did you enter the United States illegally near the town of Nogales on or about 15 September 2015?'

This one has the build of a fourteen-year-old; he is smirking shyly as he lifts himself to his feet. The earphones through which proceedings are being interpreted for him are not working. His attorney intervenes. The attorney is a big, bearded man, and, like his colleagues and the Border Patrol representatives, spends most of the hearing fingering his iPhone.

There is a delay while replacement headphones are found.

'Gentlemen,' says the judge, 'if you don't understand, please stand, or speak privately to your attorney.' Nobody stands or approaches his attorney. These are young men, self-conscious among their peers.

'Mr Manuel García, did you enter the United States illegally near the town of Nogales on or about 15 September 2015?'

There is a pause as Jesus Manuel García listens to the translation. '*Sí.*'

'You have been charged with illegal re-entry after deportation. Do you understand the charges and the maximum penalties that you are facing?'

A pause.

'*Sí.*' He glances at the men alongside him.

He is wearing a thin hooded jersey in a camouflage pattern, the kind worn by many of his fellow defendants, bought from the stalls catering to migrants on the Mexican side of the border. This is also where you buy your black plastic three-litre canteens and your electrolyte powder and the plimsolls soled with carpet that leave no prints.

'Mr Manuel García, you have agreed to plead guilty to the petty offence of illegal re-entry. In exchange, the government agrees to dismiss the more serious felony offence against you. Do you understand?'

'*Sí.*'

'Mr Manuel García, please speak up.'

There is a pause, he says it loudly this time, almost shouts. There is laughter among the other defendants.

'*Thank you*, Mr Manuel García.'

She asks him how he pleads.

He listens, and says quietly: '*Culpable.*'

'Thank you, Mr Manuel García. You are going to be deported and removed from the United States. The charge will always be on your record.'

Others, repeat offenders, are sentenced to time in jail – nine months, a year. And yet there is little palpable tension in the room. When Manuel García's group of half a dozen have received their sentences, they are led from the room. One of them wears a T-shirt with the words KEEP CALM AND CHIVE ON. I don't understand what it means. One of them is wearing a white facemask. One of them is on crutches. 'Bring 'em down!' comes a warehouse holler.

And so it goes, '*Culpable*', '*Culpable*', '*Culpable*', '*Culpable*' . . . until, after an hour, the process achieves such momentum that it seems unstoppable, and indeed once those sixty have been processed, another sixty shuffle in, and tomorrow the same, and the next day; and there is nothing in the fashion of the proceedings to give one hope it will ever ease, this filing of people. They jingle as they move, and they move slowly, not only because they are tired, their feet blistered, but because they are shackled. They are sunburned, their arms covered in scratches. They are beyond acknowledging their degradation. After one more round I sidle out into Arizona's blinding afternoon.

On the other side of the city, in the car park of Southside Presbyterian Church, fifteen men are waiting, Mexicans and Salvadoreans and Guatemalans and Hondurans. They have come here illegally; many have been deported several times. Not all of them are young. On church property they cannot be apprehended by the police or Border Patrol. Citizens of Tucson needing day labour can come here and liaise with the manager, Ereberto, who will allocate the appropriate worker or workers for a set daily fee. For six days a week the men are able to earn a living, at a fair wage and with minimal risk of arrest and deportation. (This is the perennial anxiety – that at any moment, day or night, you might be snatched and shackled and tried and sent back – not to death, necessarily, but to poverty, to chancelessness; to whatever it was that you expended so much energy, so much money, in getting away from.)

I sit among a group of them on the kerb, in the shade of the church wall. We share cigarettes and the cans of San Pellegrino lemonade I've brought. Occasionally a truck or car pulls in and one or two of the men are called away by Ereberto to go with the driver to mow a lawn or tile a roof or lay paving or clear a dead person's house. After an hour, only one guy is left, and in the absence of the others he becomes talkative. His name is Enrique. He is in his early twenties, and wears a young man's clothes – oversized baseball jersey and jeans, backwards baseball cap over his frizzy ponytail. He lives in the future, when things will be better. After all, his life today is better than it was a year ago, isn't it? He is quickened by his own words.

It is approaching 2 p.m. and the light has an astringency to it, a penetrating quality that differs from heat. The lemonade is gone, the cans lined up on the kerb between us. He is from Honduras, he says. Like thousands of others each year he crossed Mexico on the roof of *La Bestia* – the Beast – *El tren de la muerte*, the notoriously perilous network of freight trains. It took him twenty days to reach Monterrey in the north-east. He had already been deported from that city three times, he says. 'A lot of people die, you know. You can see a lot of crows beside the tracks. Sometimes on the train people are asking for water or food or money. Bad people. You don't have money, they push you off the train. I see that kind of people.'

He and two friends from Honduras caught a lift to Sonoyta on the border, and it was from there that they entered the Organ Pipe Cactus National Monument. 'No fence,' Enrique says. 'Only desert. Only desert.' It took him nine days to reach Tucson. 'For three days, no water, no food.' He became separated from his friends when he left them to search for water. 'I almost died. I was looking for them everywhere. I was screaming, asking names. And I never found them.'

He repeats himself: 'I spent three days in the desert, by myself.' He can scarcely believe it. He's not one of those wide-eyed Salvadorean farm boys with no concept of the desert's hardships, the sort who enters the desert wearing flip-flops and carrying a few cans of Coke. He had heard the stories, and there he was in the middle of one.

He found a rancher's water tank. 'I couldn't believe that. How God is.' Then he came upon a can of beans. A can of beans, sitting there in a dry wash! 'God is the only one. The *only* one. The beans were bad, but anyway I ate them. They give me energy for two more days. I got lost but then I find a town, I don't remember the name. A truck driver had a flat tyre. I helped him, and he gave me a ride to Yuma.'

From there he hopped a train to Tucson, hiding in the toilet to avoid the guard. The friends he lost in the desert? They too survived. They are in Indiana, working as roofers. He's saving for a bus ticket to join them. A car pulls in, and Ereberto is calling him, but he doesn't stand up. 'I'm feeling like I am in the middle of my road,' he says. 'God is the only one. The *only* one. The one who choose. If God wants me to go back, I'll go back.'

The thing about Border Patrol is the solitude. Once you're trained you're on your own – stationary in your truck, watching the line for eight, nine hours at a time. You need to know how to take that, John says, as we drive south from Tucson into the desert the next day. He has been well briefed; he is compassionate and reasonable. Nobody wants anyone to die out there. Billy Connolly, he says, was recently a guest. Took him and his crew up in a chopper to film the wall from above. That's a funny guy.

John himself was once a patrolman, quite senior, but he no longer spends much time in the field, and he misses it. Handholding the media and chaperoning pasty British writers is not real work, to his mind; isn't the kind of work his father would have admired.

The PR front drops an inch when we stop for a burger at a Wendy's on the Nogales road.

'If I was in their shoes? Maybe I'd want to cross, too; but I'll say this: I wouldn't cross in the desert; I wouldn't cross where it's *impossible* to carry enough water to keep me alive. I'd cross in one of the towns. Sure, you're more likely to be apprehended, but you're a heck of a lot less likely to die.'

His father? A strict man who required academic excellence of his only child. John, no scholar, was punished for his poor grades with long periods locked in his room. He did not become, therefore, a sociable boy, and grew up to experience solitude as if it were normal. It is what made him effective, before he was singled out by his employers for his manner, his diplomacy. It's a kind of strength, isn't it, being able to abide solitude?

Following Iraq and Afghanistan and Border Patrol's corresponding expansion, more and more ex-soldiers have joined up, John says. But BP is not the military; it's a very particular thing; there's nothing 'kinetic' about it (the army word: *kinesis*). The job, in essence, is to sit, to watch – and only then, sometimes, to track and to apprehend. You are a security guard (you are also an agent of punishment). To be alone, furthermore, is to be unwitnessed. It is the perennial test of the desert – a challenge to your moral core: when you can do whatever you wish, without anyone there to censure you, apart from those whom you apprehend, how do you behave?

Take a man who has seen action in one desert and put him in another, on his own. A man who's shot at nameless foreigners and seen those same foreigners shoot back. The way blood can stand on sand for minutes before it sinks in. Put him on the line.

Even in this relatively lush desert there is only so much to occupy the gaze – limestone outcrops, prickly pear, paloverde, mesquite; the sky and its carnivorous birds – before that gaze turns inwards. In the patient desert once again you will find the familiar silence, save for the radio crackle and the wheeling hawks. It is those men who either crack up, says John, or, alert to the danger within themselves, quit.

Coming back from Nogales I'd passed through the checkpoint at Amado on I-19, a dozen agents halting vehicles under a hangar-like white canopy that bridged the northbound road, a secondary line against those who had crossed the border twenty miles south. It's the scrubby badlands flanking the checkpoint that John and I search, though I'm aware it's mainly a performance for my benefit. In his green uniform he strides ahead through the gauntlet of ocotillo and cholla as if he is following a scent, blindly; he hardly hesitates. He is at ease here, and he wants to demonstrate that ease. I'm left ten feet back, hurrying to follow him up and down the bouldered arroyos. I'm soon breathless, and pause for water, my feet already blistering in their boots. The up-down terrain unsoftened by vegetation; the dazzle of the sky as you lift your gaze uphill; the heat massing in you.

For John, the trek is not, as it is for me, a mere succession of obstacles. He barely needs to attend to its physical demands; he knows an ankle-turning rock when he sees one, how to negotiate a steep scree slope (crabwise). His focus is the mark that betrays a human's recent presence; the aberration: broken or pushed-down grass, overturned stones, the slightest darkening of the sparse soil where it has been kicked. It is unforthcoming ground, this shattered limestone; even our own prints are impossible to trace when we turn back.

This is the work, then, the daily work. The country scarcely changes. A week might pass without your apprehending anyone. But that, John says, is not a week of failure. There are, he assures me, no quotas. Sure, a beautiful place to work. But frankly you don't think much about its beauty.

The ground is littered with discarded belongings. People have been coming this way for years, for generations, in fact. It is one of the great Sonoran routes, following the course of the Santa Cruz River that once, before its water was pumped and diverted from this stretch, snaked between the Baboquivari Mountains to the west and the Tumacácoris to the east. I spot a Fruity Shine lip balm and a pair of chrome-plated nail clippers. As if their owners believed they were going somewhere else entirely – a weekend break, a visit to auntie. The artefacts lie there under the ironwood tree where people rested for shade, along with empty water bottles and plastic bags and clothes. All of it slowly being drawn into the rocky ground. It is hard not to be reminded of the aftermath of a great flight; or a rush burial. I look at John with his sidearm in its holster; and, reflected in his Ray-Bans, myself in my sun hat and my rip-proof desert wear. Our breathing is audible.

Back in the truck, we roll slowly along a track, John leaning from his window as he drives, scanning the verge for prints, kick-marks, flattened vegetation. Cutting trail, they call it. This way you scarcely need to leave your vehicle, if you know the roads well enough: just note where the trail crosses the track, and drive to the next road along to see if the trail reappears there. If not, wait; they will come to you, too tired to run.

They have been here, of course, the young men in their many dozens, but not recently. High above us on a knoll, enclosed within a gleaming cyclone fence, stands one of the new line of watchtowers, designed by an Israeli defence firm. We walk to the fence and I look up at it. Its gaze is fixed southwards: radar, high-res video. It is alert to the slightest lateral movement, and in Nogales officers are stationed at their screens, ready to send agents.

In 2014, José Antonio Elena Rodríguez's mother, frustrated by the slowness of the federal investigation into his killing, sued Lonnie Swartz in federal court. It will come as a surprise when he is indicted for second-degree murder a few weeks from now (he will plead not guilty). I haven't mentioned the case but John wants to talk about it. He seems tired of toeing the PR line. A rock, if you think about it, he says, delivered with velocity and precision, is a lethal weapon. Ask the Israeli Defence Force. 'People think, "Hey, that jerk shot him for throwing a little stone."' Next to the track stands a lollipop sign warning of rough conditions ahead. 'I don't know what happened, but I know what a rock can do' – and he crouches, selects a fist-sized chunk of volcanic rock, stands and pulls back his arm and with all his strength launches it at the sign. It hits it in the centre, with an explosion of dust and a report that echoes from the hills. ∎

Emily Berry

The Remains of the Day

I am lying in the foetal position on a beach in
the east of England. Give me strength, I say
to myself, absolutely literally. England does
not exist. My enemies consider me a hard,
angry and indispensible spirit and I do not
blame them. How easy it is to do nothing,
like a spider that has crawled up a wall and
sits there on the ceiling. In late afternoon
light I am counting your favours slowly like
receipts. Imagination, morality, performance,
farewells, spending, travel, war, needs,
business, concession, feelings of entrapment
and aloneness, no rescue. Please! Melancholic
people are repugnant. I say to my detractors.
The only way you will get any answers at all is
by revealing something. And the air clings to
me like a thick layer of menthol balm, trying
to draw something out, some sickness. Who
am I to claim a spider does nothing. I can't
help noticing that my body appals you. Or
is it my mind. Some combination of the two.
And the tasks are mounting. When I regard a
person with utter contempt, when I permit the
disgust his lechery inspires to come to power
inside me I know I will never allow him to see
such a precious spectacle. May his weakness
take hold of him like a suffocating vine. My
country engulfs me. It is in a very bad state

of repair, crowded with old furniture. The smell of refuse in the stairwell. Bad odours make me curious, but I am a tired woman. There is another shore, but it will never get here. Tell me how I should love you! They are rioting in the streets, they are feverish with injustice while my neck aches from studying a number of compelling thoughts. I am being observed, it transpires, from a distance by a huge coral-coloured bird. I may be paranoid, but I feel like it's mimicking my movements. How to escape. I told you don't come back, I said, and try to go to sleep. The only way to fall asleep is to forget about being awake, but I remember everything. I had noticed the vigour and enthusiasm with which the damned were depicted being drawn down into hell. And the choir of schoolgirls singing in the background, judgemental. Your stupid, beautiful face. I kept seeing these signs that warned of 'deep excavations'. And I do not even know what it is you do to me. There is a bad thing in the mind which has not been digested; understand? This is why I have pain. My neck aches. And I am a very proud nation. The future like an insectile leg creeping over the rim of something – the horizon.

Joseph Flusfeder, *c.*1945
Courtesy of the author

VINYL ROAD TRIP

David Flusfeder

1

In the spring of 2015, at my desk in London, I received an email from a DJ/producer in Detroit. Aaron 'FIT' Siegel wanted to know the answer to two questions: was I related to Joe Flusfeder, of Lened Inc., the company that used to manufacture automated record presses in New Jersey in the 1960s and 1970s; and if so, did I know where he could find spare parts for Lened machines, because the ones at the pressing plant he uses keep breaking down.

The answer to the first question was yes: he was my father. The answer to the second was originally no. It gave me a thrill that was in part sentimental and nostalgic, and in part something else that I couldn't quite identify, to hear that the vinyl revival is being enabled on heritage machinery, that my father's machines are still in operation. I liked it too that the email had come from Detroit, with its reputation for being the exemplary ruined post-industrial American city. Aaron and I had a subsequent email correspondence in which we talked about cities and ruins and the possibilities of recovery. I told him that the Lened patent had gone into the public domain a decade or two earlier, that my father had died in 2008 and that the last time I had seen one of his machines was in 1980. The factory closed down in 1982. I wished I knew of a cache of spare Lened parts to give to Aaron. I thanked him for getting in touch. I wished him luck.

And then, a few months after the original email correspondence had subsided, I got back in touch with Aaron Siegel. I told him I was planning a visit and asked him if he would take me to Archer Record Pressing in Detroit. I had done some further research in the intervening period. I thought I might have a lead for him.

I have a framed LP from 1964. On the white label is typed the following information:

OCTOBER 29, 1964
THIS RECORD WAS MADE ON THE
FIRST DAY OF OPERATION OF THE
NEW AUTOMATIC RECORD PRESS

DESIGNED BY J. FLUSFEDER & L. PALMER
BUILT BY LENED MANUFACTURING CO., INC.
ELIZABETH, NEW JERSEY

The pianist Glenn Gould gave up performing live that year, preferring the technology of the recording studio. In 1966 he wrote: 'Whether we recognize it or not, the long-player record has come to embody the very reality of music.'

It may be embodying it again, in a surprising post-postmodern reaching for authenticity. Thomas Edison's phonograph, in which sound waves were etched onto the surface of a rotating cylinder, was invented in 1877. The first records made from polyvinyl chloride (PVC) rather than shellac were manufactured in the late 1930s, but PVC only became standard in the post-war plastics surplus that also enabled the washing-up bowl and the hula hoop. The first LP was pressed in 1948. An entire classical symphony could now be contained on a single disc. (The symphony is the unit of cultural value that the recording industry uses when it wants to boast about innovation: the compact disc's seventy-nine-minute length was chosen as being sufficient for Beethoven's Ninth.)

Like many of my father's decisions, his decision to get out of the recording business in 1982 was a shrewd one. In 1975, record sales in the USA had totalled approximately 460 million dollars. By 1978, that had gone up to around 500 million dollars, of which about two-thirds was made up of album sales and the other third of singles. But by 1982, vinyl was on the way out. Cassettes became more popular than records in 1985. CDs took over in 1989. By the 1990s vinyl records had become twentieth-century curios, a niche market kept alive by ageing audiophiles and a few purists' genres like Detroit techno.

In 2006, 900,000 records were sold in the USA. There was a slight rise to a million the following year; and then something happened. Every couple of years or so, the figure would double, so that by 2015, nearly twelve million records were sold, a rise of just under three million over 2014.

Archer Record Pressing in Detroit was one of the few plants to have survived the slump and it was now profiting from the unexpected boom.

I searched online for Leneds, and for my father's partner, and eventually I found a death notice for Leonard Palmer, who had died in Palm Beach Gardens, Florida, in 2012 at the age of ninety-five, after suffering an aneurysm on a golf course. He was survived by two children and four grandchildren. His daughter was listed under her married name along with her husband: Nina and Steve Sheldon. Nina, under her maiden name, is the National Sales Manager for Ross Ellis Packaging, which produces most of the album covers for the record industry in North America. I had come across Steve Sheldon's name before: he's the president of Rainbo Records in LA, which has maybe the largest number of working Lened machines anywhere.

And now I had a plan. I would drive from the old Lened factory in

DAVID FLUSFEDER

Elizabeth, New Jersey, then on to Detroit, where I would visit Archer's to see my father's machines in operation. And then fly to LA, to meet Steve and Nina, and broker a deal to help out Archer's.

2

I drove out of Manhattan in a rented Ford to visit my father's grave at Beth David cemetery in Elmont, which is one of those suburbs of Queens that blurs into Long Island. I was last here seven years ago, at his funeral, and, predictably, as the lack of a sense of direction is one of the few things that I unmistakably shared with my father, I couldn't find his grave. I wandered around the fancier parts of the cemetery, the tombs and vaults, some of which have windows, 'for the dead to look out', as my father said, when I drove him and my stepmother out to the cemetery to see their death plot a couple of years before he died. The comedian and provocateur Andy Kaufman is buried here, despite the rumours that he faked his own death. I didn't see his grave and I couldn't find my father's, even with the photocopied map that an anxious woman at reception had furnished me with. She'd looked my father up on the computer system and scrawled a yellow blot with a Magic Marker on the map.

'He's right there,' she said.

Except he wasn't. I'd circled around for a quarter of an hour or so before returning to the office.

'I haven't been working here long,' she told me.

She came out of the office to help me. We tramped around together for a while before I did come across a little scrub of a hedge and a stone to mark my father's grave. LOVED, MOURNED AND DEEPLY MISSED it says, which doesn't give much sense of who he was. More eloquent are the places and dates of his birth and death: WARSAW JAN. 7 1922 – NEW YORK CITY NOV. 16 2008 and his name: JOSEPH (IZIO) FLUSFEDER.

32

I've written about my father before and each time I've thought I was done with it. He was the idol and enemy of my youth, the smartest and toughest man I've ever known, and I fought against him harder than I've fought anybody.

He survived being a Jew in the German occupation of Warsaw in 1939; survived being a prisoner in a Siberian forced labour camp for sixteen months from 1940 to 1941; survived being a Polish soldier at the battle of Monte Cassino in 1944. Originally called Izio, which is a Polish version of Israel, he adopted the name George in his attempt to carve out a life as an immigrant in London after the war. He had hardly any English and his accent was heavy and when he met my mother at an East End dance organised by the Polish Ex-Servicemen's Association, she misheard his 'George' as 'Joe' and he didn't have the facility to correct her, so Joe Flusfeder he became.

Joe Flusfeder didn't like life in London. He was poor and he was made to feel 'like a dirty foreigner'. He had a flair for working with machines and was offered a place at the University of Nottingham to study engineering, but couldn't afford to take it up. Claiming experience with plastics moulding equipment, he was given a job in a spectacle-frames factory where he learned the job by doing it. Then he worked in a factory that manufactured plastic clasps for handbags. Sometimes he slept on the factory floor. Generally, he lived in rooms in east and north-east London, often sharing them with other Jewish Poles displaced by the war.

His brother, who I'm named for, was shot on a street in Warsaw by a German soldier. His father died in the death camp of Treblinka. His mother committed suicide in the Ghetto. His cousins all had similar fates and only two other members of his family survived. Searching displaced-persons camps in Italy at the end of the war, he was reunited with an aunt, his father's sister, Ruth. In London he met up with his father's brother Jerzy, who was now also called George. This George had converted to Christianity, managed to take out Dutch nationality and was on his way to live in South Africa, because he was sure that it would all happen again.

My father didn't award himself any special status for having survived. The odds had been against it. Better people than him had died. He didn't believe that there was anything meaningful to this. He had survived because he had got lucky, because the world turned in the direction it did. 'There is just a matter of simple coincidences,' he later told me. He did not like to talk about these things. *Who should I talk to?* His son, for example, was living a life of unquestionable soft privilege, and could surely not understand what might be said. And why should he seek out the company of others who had had, if not similar, at least parallel experiences? So they could congratulate each other?

In 1951, my father and mother, recently married, emigrated to the US, sponsored by his aunt Ruth, who was already in Brooklyn. In New York City, he believed, it didn't matter how foreign you were: if you were smart and worked hard, you could get on in life. He continued to work in plastics factories. At some point, in the late 1950s or early 1960s, he got a job in a small manufacturing plant in Elizabeth, New Jersey, called Lened.

The company was named for its original partners, Lenny and Ed. Of Ed I know nothing other than his name, because he was the man my father replaced. Leonard Palmer was also a Polish Jew who had come to the United States via London. He had also been in Siberia, and had also joined up with General Anders's Polish battalion that formed in the USSR and made its way through Iraq, Iran and Palestine to Italy as part of the British 8th Army.

I think Joe Flusfeder and Lenny Palmer met in London. It might have been at the factory that made spectacle frames, because Lened was involved in the grinding of lenses in its early days. And Lenny Palmer wasn't Lenny Palmer yet. He had originally been Mendel Oblengorski. At some point in the war he took on the identity of a Sicilian sailor called Leonardo Palermo in circumstances unknown, perhaps murky.

My father flourished at Lened. The story I grew up with is that in his spare time he tinkered around in a corner of the factory floor, coming up with innovations and the beginning of an invention that moved Lenny Palermo to offer him a partnership.

Joe was tall and thin; Lenny short and stocky. In their early days as partners they lived next door to each other in Fresh Meadows in Queens; each had a wife and a baby daughter. They might even have seen themselves as friends. Lenny took me to my first baseball game. When I knew him, he had close-cropped grey hair and an all-year tan because of his love for tennis and golf. Both men wore dentures. Lenny frightened me slightly with his confident robustness, but he seemed sincere in his friendliness.

My aim was to drive from Elmont to Elizabeth to see the factory building at 489 Henry Street. I was six years old and my sister was eleven when our parents separated, my mother bringing us back home to London. On subsequent summers in the States, I would spend some afternoons at Lened, the bored child hanging around a parent's workplace on school holidays. I would read in the reception area, where the two secretaries, Valerie and Barbara, worked. Valerie was large and friendly and wore sweaters with patterns on them. Barbara was younger and very thin and wore brown polo necks and slacks and big round-lensed tinted glasses. She smoked More cigarettes and was, I thought, extremely glamorous. Barbara looked Italian and had a low brittle voice and did everything quite slowly as if the world was distanced from her behind glass.

Or I would sit in Lenny's chair in the office the partners shared, with its heavy furnishings, the pair of identical mahogany desks. Lenny, who was now invariably referred to as 'that horse's ass' by my father, was seldom there. Highlights of my visits were if Pepe, the factory foreman, had any spare time for me. Pepe could sometimes be persuaded to play ping-pong in the recreation room, which was a light blue linoleum room off the main factory floor, where the machines were built. The factory floor itself was a hot, hellish place that I tried to avoid. It made me ashamedly aware of my narrow boyishness to enter this loud dirty world where bare-chested oily men laboured over machines.

I liked Pepe. He had made a dangerous crossing to leave Castro's Cuba and even though I disapproved of this, in a boy-Marxist kind of way, I forgave him. The last time I saw him was when I was sixteen and he took me drinking, the giddy rush of afternoon Heinekens, and everything he said, other than on political matters, seemed to me to be apt and wise.

Towards the end of the summer, my sister (retrieved from a romantic entanglement in the Catskills) and I would be taken by our father to All Disc, which was a pressing plant in Roselle, New Jersey, that used Lened machines. And there, in the din and the heat generated by the presses, we were given licence to gather up as many records as we could carry. Back in London each new album I bought was a sort of magical act that required much preparation. But here, at All Disc, this was the closest I could come, at the age of twelve, thirteen, fourteen, to the orgiastic. A new Lou Reed album? Put it in the cart. Cat Mother? Why not. A double-album anthology of someone called John Coltrane? I'd read about him in a Ken Kesey novel, so that went into the pile.

This was about the time when I declared that if my father thought I was going to join him in the business then he would have to think again. He didn't seem especially disappointed by the news. He didn't have a very high opinion of my likely capacities for engineering or business and he said if Lenny's son was anything like his father then he wouldn't wish a second-generation partnership on anyone. He had a higher opinion of Lenny's daughter Nina, but neither my father nor Lenny would have envisaged passing on the company to their daughters – and anyway, Nina was reported to be going off the rails at this point, working as a hot-pants-wearing waitress in a go-go bar – which made her rank in the same glamorous company as Barbara in my eyes.

My father did not have a gift for friendship. If there had ever been any sense of companionship between him and Lenny ('the horse's ass!'), Polish Jews who had survived the war, who had made the same journey, via London, to New York, then that was quickly dissipated. But my father was always complimentary about Pepe. He seemed to like him. He praised his work. Pepe was lifted away from the factory floor; his overalls were gone, he wore a business suit to work now; he took care of some of the clients, both at home and abroad. And then, abruptly, Pepe was gone. And when I asked my father what had happened, all he would say was, 'The man's a thief.'

As I drove back into Manhattan to cross over into New Jersey, I was thinking of Pepe, and wondering what it was that he had stolen, and how foolish he had been to attempt it, because he must have known that my father never forgave a slight, let alone a robbery. I was planning to go across the George Washington Bridge, through Fort Lee, where my father and his second wife had lived for a while, and across to Elizabeth. There is still a manufacturing plant at 489 Henry Street; the same one-storey brick building where Lened had been is now a factory for American Hose & Hydraulics.

The fourth-ranking attraction on TripAdvisor for things to do in Elizabeth is to take the bus to Newark Airport. Elizabeth is a run-down post-industrial rust-belt town in northern New Jersey. It hasn't recovered from the loss of its largest employer, the Singer sewing-machine factory, which closed down in 1982, the same year that Lened shut. I was already seeing plenty of post-industrial ruination on my drive out of Queens: the clumps of people idle on street corners, boarded-up buildings that had once been enterprises, the messed-up, potholed roads that the city hadn't got around to repairing.

I hadn't prepared well. It was the day of the New York Marathon, and I kept being detoured around the route. After an hour of this I was still waiting at a junction to get onto the approach road to the George Washington Bridge. I had reached the data limit on my phone, which meant that Google Maps was unavailable and I was unlikely ever to find Henry Street in Elizabeth. So I parked the car and took the subway to meet my friend Christopher for lunch.

When we first met, in our early twenties, we were both aspirant writers. Christopher was a poet, who was beginning to publish; I was a 'novelist', by intent rather than achievement. Christopher left poetry behind and has for many years been an adviser to and spokesperson for one of the richest men in the world. At the midtown office building where he works there is nothing to indicate what is transacted inside: no names on the door or in the huge white lobby with its fountain on the far wall, its travertine and glass and Mies van der Rohe chairs in the reception area, the cashmere-covered chairs in the executive suite.

The only thing on display, other than New York City itself through the office windows, is an installation created by James Turrell, sited across two floors. An elegant ovoid, it's one of the artist's *Ganzfelds*, an immersive experience in which your entire field of vision is solid and undifferentiated, with no horizon. We stood inside it and looked up, climbed to the next floor and leaned vertiginously over the edge. The lighting was set to blue, and it felt impossible not to have intimations of the infinite.

'This might be the opposite of Detroit,' I said, when we'd stepped out of the installation.

'This might be why Detroit is broke,' Christopher said.

This is how the world works: your rust belt is his travertine wall. Nietzsche wrote, 'Mankind is not a whole; it is an inextricable multiplicity of ascending and descending life-processes . . . the strata are twisted and entwined together . . . Decadence . . . belongs to all epochs of mankind: refuse and decaying matter are found everywhere.'

It takes about eleven hours to drive from Manhattan to Detroit, where, according to its current reputation, a lot of that decaying matter is to be found. I'd read about lawlessness and murders and was determined to arrive in daylight. I left Manhattan at 6.30, stopping for breakfast in a diner in a small town in Pennsylvania, where I sat across from the Fire Chief, Paul. I knew he was called Paul and that he was the Fire Chief because he was wearing a blue T-shirt that said so. Paul the Fire Chief was magnificent. He was a big man, balding, with a large grey moustache and the appetite of a king. I watched, with some measure of awe, Paul consume bacon, sausages, fried potatoes, waffles, pancakes, scrambled eggs, toast and jelly, and a little white bowl of what I later realised were grits. There was magnificent amplitude to his appetite, and watching Fire Chief Paul consume his breakfast put me in a very good mood. Getting back onto the road, I admired the scenery, the November sun that was colouring everything green and gold, flashing through the trees like the lights of a patrol car.

I got over my guilt that I hadn't made it to Elizabeth, that I'd allowed poor planning and the New York Marathon and telephone data usage and James Turrell to deflect me from it. Joe Flusfeder wouldn't have minded. He was not a sentimental man. He never declared any feelings or curiosity or interest in Elizabeth, or Berkeley Heights, where he had, as they used to say, begun to 'raise a family'. He had been in Elizabeth solely because of work, because Lenny Palermo and the unknown Ed had happened to set up a factory there. He chose, when he could afford to, to live in Manhattan. Elizabeth and Fort Lee and Berkeley Heights and Fresh Meadows, like London, like Monte Cassino or Siberia or Warsaw, were unavoidable steps on his way.

I turned left at Toledo and headed into Detroit. It was still daylight.

3

Detroit used to be the 'most modern city in the world, the city of tomorrow', as the journalist and poet Matthew Josephson wrote in 1929. This is the city of the American automobile industry, where Henry Ford, who had previously worked for Thomas Edison's Illuminating Company, designed the production line. It's the city of Motown records and techno music. Charles Lindbergh and Aretha Franklin were born here; Harry Houdini died here.

In the 1950s, nearly two million people lived in Detroit, making it the fourth-largest city in America after New York, Los Angeles and Chicago. Now there are fewer than 700,000 inhabitants, and it's the eighteenth largest, with a population just slightly bigger than El Paso's. The city filed for bankruptcy in December 2013, with debts of around $18 billion.

Detroit's fortunes have failed and recovered before. Since its earliest days, as a French fort and fur-trading post on the straits (*le détroit*) of Lake Erie, it has been the setting for alarming tales of violence and ruin and fire. The first time the place burned to the ground was when the Americans took the stronghold from the French. In World War II, the conversion of automobile factories to the manufacture of tanks and aircraft lifted Detroit's fortunes after the stock market crash and the Great Depression. The city motto is *Speramus melior; resurget cineribus*: 'We hope for better days; it shall rise from the ashes.' As they say at the techno museum: 'Say nice things about Detroit!'

Berry Gordy modelled Motown on what he had seen when he worked at Ford. 'We took the assembly line approach. We had a charm school and a production room, and we had classes, and we had producers, and we had writers . . . At the plant, cars started out as just a frame, pulled along on conveyor belts until they emerged at the end of the line – brand-spanking-new cars rolling off the line. I wanted the same concept for my company, only with artists and songs and records.'

This is acted out in the 1965 promotional video for 'Nowhere to Run' in which Martha Reeves and the Vandellas shimmy and dance and mime around the production line at the Ford River Rouge factory at Dearborn. They climb into a car and the song finishes as the completed Ford Mustang rolls off the line.

The Rouge is now a museum. So is the Motown building. 'The Sound of Young America' left for LA in 1974. James Joyce said that Rome reminded him of a man who made a living by exhibiting his grandmother's corpse. Detroit could go the same way. It can be eerie being in a more than half-deserted city, where many buildings have crumbled or been demolished or stripped of anything that can be sold, while photographers and film crews take artful shots in the urban prairies, where wild grass grows on empty lots.

But I am resolved to look for ascending processes and not to peddle in ruins porn, even though I was meeting my email contact Aaron Siegel at the Astro Coffee Shop on Michigan Avenue, which stands opposite the abandoned Michigan Central Station. The train station, once the largest in America, was shut down in 1988. It's owned by Manuel Moroun, who also owns the bridge into Canada – the station has been left to rot while Moroun gets richer on the tolls for the bridge. We're in Corktown, which, as its name implies, used to be an Irish neighbourhood; then it fell emptier, and now there are slow-food barbecue joints and artisan-beer bars frequented by young people who have come to live in Detroit because rent is cheap and the ruins are kind of beautiful and art and music is being made here.

There is time to contemplate the ruins – there is time to contemplate most things – when waiting for a coffee at the Astro. The barista builds it sacramentally, touching your coffee with eternity while dripping it slowly through. You look around for some diversion and what you might notice is the lack of diversity, because, in a city that's over 80 per cent black, on my three visits to the Astro, I saw only one person of colour in there.

This isn't a piece about race, but it's impossible to avoid the subject when writing about America, particularly American cities – and Detroit is an extreme example of an American city, albeit an especially anomalous one. It's so far north that Canada is to its south, yet, because of the car industry and the music scene, generations of people from the south have come to live here looking for work. Members of the Funk Brothers, Motown's session musicians, were as likely to come from Mississippi and Tennessee as Michigan.

Riots broke out in Detroit in 1943 and 1967. John Lee Hooker sang about the latter one in 'The Motor City is Burning' ('My hometown burning down to the ground / Worser than Vietnam'), which fades on Hooker half singing, half saying, 'Let's get out of here.'

A lot of people who could afford to took him at his word. Most of the older white people I spoke to in Detroit lived 'in the suburbs'. Playing poker at the MotorCity Casino, I declared my intention to walk the following morning to the Detroit Institute of Arts. The people of colour who were at my table assured me that it wasn't much more than fifteen minutes. The white people shook their heads. The player to my right, a retired 8th-grade algebra teacher said, 'I'll pick up your body in the afternoon.' This is a car city, built to make cars, and to drive them. The mass transit system is rudimentary at best. More and more people, particularly the younger incomers, are using bicycles. The only other people I ever saw walking, apart from in the business district, looked like they were doing so because they had no choice. None of them was white.

Nothing happened to me, or threatened to, on my walk to the DIA.

My guide to the Diego Rivera mural there, a masterpiece of industrial process, commissioned by Edsel Ford, was also a retired teacher. She praised the new mayor of Detroit, for his 'ideas' and his 'initiatives'. Mike Duggan is the first white mayor of Detroit in forty years. As Aaron Siegel says, 'The "New Detroit" means "White Detroit" – making it okay for white people.'

Aaron arrived at the Astro about the same time my coffee did. He's wiry and energetic and in the Detroit spirit is busy making things. He makes music and produces it, and distributes other people's music, and all of it is being pressed at Mike Archer's plant.

To make records all you need is space and air and water. And raw PVC pellets to feed into the machine. And, of course, the machines themselves. There are approximately 225 record presses left in the world. Some of them were designed by my father, and Mike Archer has three of them.

I'd last seen a Lened machine in operation in the summer of 1980. Archer Record Pressing is familiar, a factory just like Lened, one storey, low-slung, on a light industrial street of similar sorts of enterprises, most of which have closed down.

I felt a goofy sort of unearned pride to see these forty-year-old machines with their red Lened nameplates and huge hydraulic presses, taller than their operators, made of grey-green steel with rubber tubing curving hot and cold water inside them. A record machine is really two machines, an extruder to squeeze the raw plastic pellets into a plug to which the press itself applies 1,800 pounds of pressure at 320 degrees Fahrenheit to inscribe the grooves. No concession is made to aesthetics. A record press as designed by my father is pure function. Button pressed: PVC plug moved to the plates that contain the negative imprints of the master disc; plug flattened; labels applied; hole punched. After the disc is pressed, and cooled, it is shunted along to the trimming-station part of the machine, where the excess vinyl is sliced away.

It was early November when I visited. Detroit was having an unlikely heatwave, and it was crazily hot on the street and therefore worse in the factory. They were sweating heavily inside the plant, Mike Archer and his two employees: Kenny is the machine operator, and Andy, who is a techno fan from Indiana and considers it an honour to be working at Archer's, does just about everything. At the moment I arrived, that meant mopping up a pool of water because one of the Leneds had sprung a leak and a third of the factory's production was shut down for the day.

Like all pressing plants, Archer's turns away a lot more business than it takes. Mike Archer has set himself the rule of only accepting orders from pre-existing customers and new customers from Detroit. Even so, the waiting list for new orders is about three months.

He took me through all the problems that can go wrong with pressing a record.

'Every step of the way, cutting the lacquer, plating, pressing – the main thing we fight and that most pressing plants fight is non-fill, where the grooves don't completely fill, and that'll be noisy. You can have problems with the material, you know, it can be crappy material. And you know, you have a problem, the question is, Where does the problem actually lie? Say I'm having non-fill, how do you cure that? You run the dies a little hotter. But don't run them too hot, you start warping records, right? You fix one problem, you cause another problem. People realise, these are records, they're not going to be perfect, you're going to have a tick, you're going to have a pop. That's part of the personality of vinyl too.'

I asked him if the machinery has a personality too. How would he characterise the Lened?

'I like it,' he said. 'It's very linear.'

I wasn't entirely sure what he meant by that, but I took it as a compliment and I smiled at him and he smiled back; two men in their fifties, one of whom had embraced his father's business, the other who had turned his back on it.

The factory was set up by Mike Archer's grandfather in 1965. Mike trained as an accountant and never expected to go into the family business, but he worked here for a summer twenty years ago and never left.

'Things were really going downhill in the early nineties. But we still had Detroit techno music.'

It was that very Detroit sound, which has its source in the astro-funk of George Clinton mixed with the man-machine music of Kraftwerk, that kept record-pressing alive in Detroit, and kept these Leneds in operation.

The next day Aaron took me to the techno museum, which is just around the corner from the Motown museum. Upstairs a young jazz-saxophone player was rehearsing. Outside on the stoop a Berlin artist on a month-long residency was taking in the rays.

Inside, away from the studio on the ground floor, it's just like Motown, curating its own history. At the Motown museum there'd been an extrovert young enthusiast to take the tour party around the glass cases of photographs and artefacts. Here, I had Aaron Siegel, who pointed out photographs of the car ('The Punisher') Mike Banks drove in street races against Colombian cocaine dealers. 'He built this studio with the prize money.' Here's a photograph of Jeff Mills and Robert Hood and Mike Banks DJ-ing at a club in Berlin in 1991, their faces masked, because this is the headquarters of the strand of techno called Underground Resistance ('music from adversity'), and there is no star system – individuals are subsumed in the process. And here are artefacts from all the stages of the production of a record, from the original tape to the cut lacquered master disc, to the negatives that are used to create the stampers from which the actual records are pressed. And there is the Archer logo in a corner of one of the cases.

An inner sleeve in one of the vitrines has the caption: 'Every new record equals new hope . . . This record represents a hope, a dream and a future & truly that's what music means for us here in Detroit.'

These words, signed off with the motto 'Vinyl forever' could have been drawn from Motown's mission statement except for Underground Resistance's anti-author (and anti-authoritarian) stance. They're credited to 'The unknown writer'.

'Vinyl forever'. It's the Detroit ethos, of work and process.

In 1942, in one of his snappier lines, Theodor Adorno observed that 'The Ford model and the model hit song are all of a piece'. He saw this formulaic standardisation as a bad thing – as if, in a Romantic way, true music, great music, high art, heeds no prescriptions, oversteps all boundaries, in the great rush of its creator's genius.

Twenty years later, words like 'plastic' and 'manufactured' were coming to be used, in a way that Adorno would recognise, to deride the 'culture industry'. They have those connotations still. 'Plastic' remains an easily reached-for synonym for artificial or cheap or valueless. Or indeed hazardous: the raw PVC that feeds into the Lened's extruder comes from Thailand or China, because it has a lead content that many countries consider dangerous (and the use of chlorine in the production of PVC prompted Greenpeace to rank it as the most environmentally unfriendly polymer).

But say 'vinyl' rather than 'plastic' and the reference is to something authentic rather than bogus or wrong. I spoke to the Atlanta-based punk musician Matt Gibson Hatcher, who said, 'For a lot of DIY musicians including myself, vinyl is a return to reality.'

And that 'reality' is a very personal one: it's this record, *my* record, which wears its own history, which sounds its own history, which is mine. Listening to music on vinyl, we're also hearing all the previous occasions when we've listened to it before. With a digital recording, the only mediation is the system on which the music is being played.

For example, I still can't listen to Al Green's 'Here I Am (Come and Take Me)' without experiencing the scratch that my copy of the record had on it, the little stop, click and shuddering over the groove at the beginning of the middle eight. To hear the song 'whole' is not the right experience – and nor does it feel right, or 'authentic', you might say, to listen to the album song by song, all of it on CD, with or without bonus tracks, or streamed on Spotify or on YouTube (Full Album).

Vinyl lays bare its own process, those pops and ticks, the imperfections that were stamped into it, the ones we add later in relationship with it. And if Detroit teaches us anything, it's to respect process and production as much as invention.

Before I left Archer's, Andy, who had overheard some of my conversation with Mike, asked to have his picture taken with me. It took a moment for me to work out why he would want to do that.

'It's not me,' I said. 'I had nothing to do with this. I didn't design these machines.'

'But it's your genetics,' he said.

He waited politely for me to stand beside him.

'Sometimes you wonder if they play them or just look at them . . .' Mike Archer said, walking past a freshly pressed record, a red seven-inch, sliding into its stack. He took our picture on Andy's iPhone.

4

Travelling around America can do strange things to one's state of being. By the time I'd flown into Los Angeles I had become inhabited by a kind of Andy Warhol attitude of mind: Everything is sort of okay, everything is sort of great. In England, I spend a great amount of emotional energy being irritated. But here, in LA, I was never irritated. Walking with my friend Bruno on the beach at Santa Monica, we passed the actor Harrison Ford sitting on a bench in shorts and T-shirt and floppy hat taking in the sun. And that was fine. And the movie executive a few doors down from Bruno's house, who has the mock-up police car in his driveway, with its lights perpetually flashing at night, because the executive's wife fears their proximity to a 'bad' neighbourhood (and 'bad' in this context predictably means African American), even though the nearest 'bad' neighbourhood is about five miles away, well, that's fine too. I'm glad to hear what actually happened between Lened and Pepe. And for my father's achievement and, indeed, his sexual habits, to be called into question, well then I guess that's going to have to be okay too.

When this all started, with Aaron's email, there had been the rush of sentimentality – my father, his machines, my youth, records, vinyl, cities. I had enjoyed remembering Lenny and Pepe and Valerie and Barbara. I had not expected to be sitting in a kitchen in suburban Los Angeles with Nina Palmer, the daughter of Lenny Palmer, who before that had been Leonardo Palermo and before that Mendel Oblengorski.

But first I went to see her husband. Steve Sheldon runs Rainbo Records in Canoga Park, on the outskirts of LA. He came to work here over forty years ago and now runs the company. Mike Archer has three Leneds; Steve Sheldon has fifteen and he used to have more. This is a much bigger operation than Archer's. We sat in his office, which had closed-circuit screens showing all the different areas of the factory, where the lacquers are cut, where art is designed, and the enormous CD-manufacturing machine, which looks like a hospital of the future imagined in 1999. He glanced at the screens and settled back and gave me the overview on the vinyl revival.

'So here's how I view it: ten, fifteen years ago, we were pressing for the audiophile fanatics and the guys who just had to have analogue. And then there used to be the DJ pools. So that was what we were pressing through the 1990s and the 2000s. If we were pressing fifteen to twenty thousand records in a week that would be a lot. That's how slow it got. We needed space for the CD equipment so we got rid of fourteen presses in 1994. This all started in 2009, we saw an increase, 2010 a little bit more, 2011, my youngest son went to NYU. We moved him into the dorm and a bunch of the kids who were moving into the floor brought record players and I was blown away – his room-mate brought his record player with about fifty records. When he found out that I made records, I was like the god. So it continued to grow and then 2012–13 it really started to boom. Kids were talking to each other, they were buying these turntables and now they were building their collections. So catalogue items, the Beatles, Pink Floyd, Led Zeppelin, all the old titles, these kids owned record players and now they wanted records.'

I was surprised. Why not go to record shops, buy used records, second-hand?

Second-hand stuff got depleted, Steve said. 'The majors ordered big quantities of those inventory titles, the catalogue titles. So that's kind of what happened in 2014 and the beginning of 2015. So the reorder pattern has slowed down.

'New artists. Take Taylor Swift, we press Taylor Swift for Universal. Her new album which came out in January, double-album vinyl set, it sold I don't know how many CDs, but the vinyl is up to about 150,000, which is a very respectable number for vinyl. That's not going to go away but the catalogue stuff is going to slow down.'

And now? If you were pressing a maximum of 20,000 records a week ten years ago, how many are you manufacturing now?

'We're averaging about 140,000 per week.'

In my Andy Warhol way, I couldn't avoid saying, Wow. That's quite a difference.

'Yes it is and I wish we could make more. From vinyl to cassettes to CDs to DVDs, we went back in a big way to vinyl, because we didn't get rid of our equipment. We had twenty presses, now we have fifteen. And a couple more in the warehouse that we kept for parts and that I'm now rebuilding. I probably did that with thirty or forty presses over the years and I wish I had every one of those back.'

Mike Archer's turnaround time is twelve weeks; Steve Sheldon's is even longer. 'A new client? We're telling them about thirty weeks. If they want to wait, we'll take the order. Most of them don't, obviously. They'll try to find something else, maybe they're successful. So that's how I handle new clients. With existing clients, what I do, to be fair, is, like if Universal is 15 per cent of my business before, before this happened – ' and by *this* he means the astonishing upsurge in demand ' – then they're still 15 per cent of my business. I've increased my business so they're getting more product, but I'm keeping their percentages because I want to be fair to the independents and I want to be fair to myself, because this isn't going to be here forever.'

If you go into a record store now, you'll see that new records boast about their weight: 180 grams! Hi-fidelity! I asked Steve if he shared my doubt that the weight of a record has much bearing on the sound quality. He shrugged. 'It doesn't really matter that much anyhow, if they're playing them on those Crosley decks.'

I quoted the figure that Mike Archer had given me, that 35 per cent of new records don't get listened to. That the buyer just wants the object to fetishise and instead plays the mp3 download.

'I've heard that figure. We've had a lot of discussion over that number. But me personally, I think half of everything out there doesn't get listened to.'

A Lened press cost $40,000 forty years ago. Steve could get about $50,000 now if he wanted to sell one of them. By contrast, the flashy immense CD machine cost Rainbo over a million dollars a little more than ten years ago. He'd be lucky to get the price of a Lened for it. 'The presses are on twenty-four hours a day, six days a week. We work them hard,' Steve said.

I was glad to hear that. My father would approve. I was still pushing for some sort of identification of the machine with the man, wondering if the spirit of Joe Flusfeder inheres in his design in a way it never quite did in his human relationships. Seven years before he died, my father suffered a stroke. A massive effort of will gathered what was left of him to himself; it was an astonishing, quite naked display of pure life force fighting to go on living. The language centre of his brain was damaged, which meant that his powers of comprehension and expression were impaired, particularly in his use of nouns. When searching for a noun that was stubbornly unavailable to him, he would usually settle for 'unit', which was the word he had traditionally used to denote a Lened press.

I asked Steve why Rainbo had bought Leneds, rather than Hamiltons say, or SMTs, the two other American manufacturers of automated presses. It was his old boss Jack Brown who had bought them, having been recommended them by Horace Waddell at a rival pressing plant.

'Jack got on really well with Lenny. Not so well with your father. Horace Waddell had the same situation. He would only talk to Lenny. Horace was a very blunt kind of guy. He would basically tell you to go fuck yourself if he felt like it. And I remember him telling Lenny, "Don't ever let Joe call me again." '

I chuckled politely in a that-old-bastard sort of way, and changed the subject: So will you help out Mike Archer? Do you have spare parts?

'We're having parts machined and we're replicating parts. Yeah. He should get in touch with me. I don't know them at all. I know most of the other plants.'

Job done. I had bridled a little at his references to my father. Even though I feel I have the right to be plain-speaking about him, I don't always extend the privilege to everybody else. But Steve had shown me a very hospitable combination of kindliness and respect and candour. And after all, I reminded myself, I was in the other side's camp now, so to speak, talking to the son-in-law of the horse's ass. They're bound to be partial here.

When I'd last met Nina, she had been a teenager who wore hot pants professionally. Our fathers shared an office, with heavy identical mahogany desks. Now she's a successful businesswoman, who is also exerting herself to make life in the recording industry more congenial to women. We fell into an immediate accord, with our overlapping memories of our fathers. As we sat in her kitchen, drinking coffee, it felt like we were family members enjoying a long-withheld reunion, taking turns to offer memories of the past.

Nina remembered the time they'd moved to a new town in New Jersey, the only Jewish family on a Catholic street, and her parents went away on holiday to Puerto Rico with a couple who were probably connected to the Mafia. When they got back the incipient friendship was over and Lenny realised it was time to Americanise his surname from Palermo to Palmer.

Lenny's domestic routine was absolute. He ate breakfast at seven, lunch at noon, supper at five thirty. And she remembered her father's skill with machinery, his obsessive nature; home was 'all valves and vacuum seals'.

'Whatever he did he wanted to be the best. My dad, I remember on the inside, yours on the outside, he was the gentleman of the pair, always better dressed.'

I didn't quite follow this inside-outside thing, and although my father had expensive tastes I didn't really think of him as being that much of a dandy, but I asked her if she knew why they fell out. I told her I had some memory of Lenny trying to make things better with Joe, and my father always resisting.

'They were both such strong quirky guys. A bit righteous and insecure and so secure at the same time. My dad would work Monday, Tuesday and half-day Wednesday, and your dad would work the other half-day Wednesday, Thursday and Friday. Bizarre. And I do remember some physical altercation and some heavy object being thrown resulting in a big dent or mark in one of their desks. Think perhaps that was when they decided not to see each other. But I do not know what caused the issue. I guess it will be a mystery forever . . .'

Talking of mysteries, I asked her about Pepe and if she knew what it was that he had stolen. And why? It seemed such an unlikely thing for him to do. He'd been the foreman, he was now almost a partner.

'He didn't steal anything, but he made the fatal error. He decided that Lened couldn't function without him and so gave the dads an ultimatum: either they gave him a percentage of the business or he would quit. Knowing our fathers, ultimatums were not a good negotiating tool! They told him no deal, gave him a 100,000-dollar severance pay and he moved to Florida and opened a McDonald's.'

So that was the 'thievery': Pepe presumed to lay claim to some of Joe's company. At least on that matter he and his partner were in accord.

'In the beginning, they made the perfect partnership I think. My dad doing most of the inventing and your dad doing the purchasing and selling.'

Whoa. Hold back there.

Nina might have mistaken my silence for lack of comprehension.

'Your father was the collector,' she said. 'He was the financial guy, the wheeler-dealer. Without him Lened probably wouldn't have lasted. My dad was the inventor.'

Oh. But that's not what I heard. My father was the inventor. Yours was the horse's ass.

In each of our versions of history, mine and Nina's, our father is the principal inventor. Why should that be so important? And why do I want my father's version to be right? In Nina's world view, her father was the natural inventor, driven always to tinker around with machines; my father was the wheeler-dealer, the tough negotiator, the flashy dresser.

What had happened to Joe Flusfeder's family in the war was an event of such unthinkable enormity that there was nothing he could do against it other than to boycott German products. He could though take his revenge on having felt excluded from Englishness by staying at Claridge's when he visited London. Whatever the best was that was for sale, he had a right to buy it. Nina's father Lenny, on the other hand, lived frugally, repaired furniture with duct tape and felt it was important to pass on as much as possible of the wealth he had made. When my father died, my stepmother was shocked at how little money they had left.

Could my father have forced his name onto the patent? To both Mike Archer and Steve Sheldon I'd shown copies of the four old patent documents that Lened had filed between 1965 and 1972. Two of them relate to the New Automatic Record Press, the machine that made their fortunes. On those, the inventors are listed, as they are on the record their first machine produced, as J. Flusfeder and L. Palmer. The later two are for other machines. Looking at a 1972 patent, Steve said, 'This was one of their rare duds'. On those the order of names is reversed: L. Palmer and J. Flusfeder. I'd asked if the priority of names referred to who was the principal inventor and Steve said, 'I couldn't say.'

I'm seeing my father through his partner's eyes – the tough operator who no one liked, and who enabled Lenny's smartness to come to market – but in my father's story Lenny was the horse's ass whom he was happy to see sidelined into ineffectual new products ('one of their rare duds'), because at least then he couldn't do much damage . . . Lenny could be allowed out to talk to Horace Waddell for some smiling glad-handing, he could do that with his seemingly sunny personality. Joe would have allowed him out for customer relations, but not for the deal-making, he wouldn't have trusted him to do that.

Doubt had changed the temperature in the room.

In a perhaps misjudged attempt to repair our intimacy I told Nina about a conversation my father and I had had, long after the Lened

factory had closed down. I had asked him about affairs he'd had
when he was married to my mother. Openness of this kind did not
come easily to him. We had reached an unspoken understanding that
we would not discuss any overlap there might have been between his
first and his second wives, but in return for this tact of mine he was
required to give some kind of honest answer.

'A colleague at work,' he finally said.

I reported this to Nina. It felt like a less difficult question than who
had invented what. Maybe, she said, it was someone at All Disc. 'The
two companies worked very closely together, at least at the beginning.'

'I always assumed it was Barbara,' I said, thinking of her brown
sweaters and her tinted glasses and her More cigarettes. 'A "colleague
at work" would have been code for secretary.'

I couldn't interpret Nina's expression. Nor did I understand her
answer.

'If it was, then Valerie would have known about it. She might have
made it happen.'

She was reluctant to explain but I pushed her on this.

'When I worked at Lened, it was at a difficult time in my life,'
she said. 'I'd dropped out of school, I'd been working at a go-go bar.
I broke up with a guy, I moved back home. And I got a job at Lened,
as a bookkeeper. My dad was a tough guy to work for, but it was
great, it brought us together, but I didn't work there under my own
name, I didn't want special privileges, didn't want other people to
know my dad was the boss.'

'And Valerie . . . ?'

'She was into weird stuff.'

'What kind of weird?'

'Whips, handcuffs, she had this whole room in her house . . .
And she had this biker boyfriend, they got up to these things. It was
kinky . . . Not my kind of thing.'

'She invited you to take part?'

'Yeah, but it wasn't my kind of thing.'

Talk about patents receded from my mind. Was it my father's

kind of thing? Did they do this kind of thing in the early 1970s in New Jersey? I'd always thought of him as somewhat prudish. Was he a willing participant in Valerie's sex dungeon? Or, slightly less unlikely but much creepier, he was having an affair with Barbara and Valerie was the presiding genius of it all, maybe Barbara had to visit Valerie and her biker boyfriend afterwards, report back. Maybe whatever she did with my father was merely foreplay to the real activity?

I don't believe that there's necessarily a sexual undercurrent, or meaning, to all human motivation. My father operated at a primal level, in which to be alive was the primary good, and to succeed over other people was the next, and possibly final, consideration. He once told me a story of when he was a prisoner in Siberia, of the camp for women that was just across the way. The inmates there taunted the men, standing at windows with their skirts raised. One woman looked across at him, rubbing herself with a home-made dildo, a sock filled with salt.

'They offered a deal. They wanted us to come over there, you know, pleasure them, food for sex.'

'And?'

He shrugged. He made his smile that referred to no humour, just the awful comedy of it all.

'We couldn't perform. No function left. I wanted to. I wanted the food! But, nothing doing.'

Nina asked after my mother. Her family always had a loyalty to her, to my father's first marriage, and maybe to the man my father had been back then, or at least seemed to be promising to become. And maybe the partners' arguments had nothing to do with business at all, maybe it was Lenny's disapproval at my father being unfaithful to my mother, for allowing that marriage to end.

I couldn't keep from thinking about the authorship issue. It is possible that my father took credit that he didn't deserve, 'the operator' muscling, wanting his name first, maybe arguing that alphabetical order should decide priority, Lenny agreeing, to keep an uneasily shifting peace. And it is also possible that 'the horse's ass' didn't even deserve that, his ineffectual tinkering a forlorn attempt to prove that he could do it too. It is possible that it was my father's mind – the imagination without sensibility, the capacity or predilection he had to stare clear-eyed at things in their harshest light – which designed that machine with its linear quality, stripped down to its essentials like a Hemingway sentence, and that the only reason Lenny's name is on those first patents at all is that it was his company, there was no getting around that.

Or it could have been actually collaborative, a true partnership, at least for a while, and this is what I'm going to choose to believe: Joe saw the big picture, he had a flair for systems; he might have devised the outline that Lenny the engineer filled in.

Regardless of who did what, part of their enmity would have been the fact that Lenny had once been my father's boss. To have had authority over him, to have been in a position to help him – and to have done so – would have been unforgivable.

Whatever caused the partners to fall out, Joe and Lenny are both dead. There's no one left to ask.

When Joe – or George as he would have been then – met his uncle in London soon after the war, Jerzy had somehow integrated himself into a Dutch trade mission and had cast his Jewishness behind, and his Polishness, on his way to an invented life in South Africa. 'What he was basically saying,' my father said, looking back at this fifty years later, 'was, "You should erase everything that happened in the past." '

Joe Flusfeder didn't try to do this. He changed his first name but kept his odd surname, which he would always have to spell out, as I do, as my children have to do, to any new acquaintances.

It feels appropriate that they made their livings in plastic moulding technology. The plastics industry, particularly after the war, in the aftermath of that great dispersal, of violent endings and enforced new beginnings, was more open to exiles than most. My father – Joe/George/Izio – and his partner – Lenny/Leonardo/Mendel – were, if not quite self-made, at least self-moulded men.

And if identity is not quite so fixed, then after a while there is perhaps something comic or even hapless about an ageing man still trying to deal with the questions of his youth and his not-knowing about his father. When does it become unseemly, these excavations into the family past?

Already I can look a little nervously over my own shoulder, at my son, and wonder quite what he is thinking when he looks at me like that. ■

'The desert is the most painful journey,' said an explorer I met last year. 'Anyone who crosses is between life and death.'

His fellow adventurer agreed. 'One thing that scared me was the dry bones. Were they donkeys or camels starved of water? Or something else?'

A Gambian and a Nigerian, they were among 560 men I found incarcerated in the Libyan port city of Misrata, categorised not as travellers but criminals for leaving West Africa and trying to reach Europe across the Sahara and the Mediterranean. The accounts of such journeys – the dangers of the desert followed by the perils of the sea – are included not in anthologies of travel writing, but police and immigration authority reports. They tell of torture, rape, despair and a determination to keep going that defies the understanding of the comfortable.

These are the pioneers of our day, discovering new lands just as Mungo Park did in the great age of European exploration of Africa.

'Whatever difference there is between the Negro and European, in the conformation of the nose, and the colour of the skin, there is none in the genuine sympathies and characteristic feelings of our common nature,' wrote Park in 1799, six years before he came to grief on the rapids while searching for the source of the River Niger.

Yet, more than two centuries later, difference remains in the value we assign to the direction of travel and the reason for setting out. Maybe we shy away from this kind of story because it is so harrowing – the lightness of touch we have come to expect from Redmond O'Hanlon or Bruce Chatwin is rarely to be found in such stories. But a terrifying journey of necessity may be more compelling than one of choice, and a Western reader might find how such travellers view us more fascinating than our own tales of far-off lands.

We need a new genre of travel writing, gleaned from the stories refugees and migrants tell housing officials, charity centres, immigration officers, health workers and school admissions staff. Not everything said or written would be true – but exaggeration and elision have long been hallmarks of travel writing. Maybe a new style could escape the bureaucratic language to which these dramatic journeys are usually reduced.

One of the men I met in Misrata, an Eritrean called Yonatan, listed the countries through which he had travelled: Sudan, South Sudan, Uganda, Kenya, Ethiopia. He had moved on foot and by bus, jeep, truck and donkey. Furtively, so the guards could not see, he showed me the Bible he carried, secreted in a small leather pouch. Since escaping prison in Libya he has notched up Italy, Sweden and everywhere in between. The stories of the millions like Yonatan trying to reach Europe are the travellers' tales that define our times. ■

The first time I ever visited a place I'd read about in a travel book was when my family took a holiday in Hong Kong in 1993. I was twelve, and I'd found and read a yellowing edition of Ian Fleming's *Thrilling Cities* only the previous year. In Hong Kong, the inaugural stop on his itinerary, Fleming received a Tiger Balm massage, messed around with chopsticks, played fan-tan in Macau, and discussed the Bretton Woods agreement. Given my age, I could partake in only one of these thrills. I concentrated hard, during my trip, to see if the city felt in any way like Fleming's Hong Kong, but in vain. Much later, I realised how foolish it was to imagine that my experience of a place would chime perfectly with a travel writer's. It would have been just as silly to expect my schooldays to be duplicates of Tom Brown's, or my first brush with true love to resemble Romeo's.

Those who like to sound the death knell for travel literature often portray the world as over-described. We have an Internet flooded with people conveying the details of their awful flights, the views outside their seaside cottages, their lunches in wherever, their holidays doing whatever. They do this through blog posts, tweets, Flickr, Facebook notes and Instagram; in private, they send Snapchats and Vines and WhatsApp photos. This doesn't even take into account the sheaves of glossy travel magazines, the supplements of newspapers, television shows and online travel forums. Between them, these media seem to have captured every square inch of our planet, every ounce of every conceivable human experience. What more could possibly be left to say?

But that way lies fallacious thought. It presumes that our destinations are frozen in time, which couldn't be further from the truth. Forests change through the seasons, and then over years. Cities expand. Populations dwindle. New cultures mix into old. The heat grows, the glaciers melt. The Hong Kong that Fleming visited in 1959 could never have been the Hong Kong that subsequent travellers discovered for themselves. The literature of travel describes the world as it is – but only as it is in its instant, as it appears to the particular sensibility of the passing witness.

For that is the other aspect of travel writing that has begun frequently to be overlooked – that it has as much to do with the beholder as the beheld. The writer filters her surroundings through her temperament, distilling something richer and more meaningful in the process. This is, after all, the most fundamental kind of literary work. Every writer's account of her journeys will necessarily be unique. If anything, in fact, the avalanche of superficial information out there will only inspire writers of merit to dig deeper and think harder. As long as there are writers, and as long as they stir occasionally out of their houses, there will be travel writing worth reading. ■

ANOTHER GREAT LEAP

Justin Jin

Introduction by A Yi

TRANSLATED FROM THE CHINESE BY LU NAN

My father, a 72-year-old former state-owned company employee and businessman, passed away recently and we returned his ashes to his home town, a small village called Ai's Creek to the south of Fan, a town in Jiangxi Province. A man will only return to his birthplace in the countryside when he is dead. This is our reality.

Our branch of the 'Ai' clan (my birth name is Ai Guozhu) migrated to Ai's Creek during the Ming dynasty. Today, among the ninety-six male descendants in my family, only two remain there. One is very old; the other, who is much younger, also owns a place in the local town where his wife and children live. The reason why he stays in Ai's Creek is because he wants to look after the farmland, which has been deserted by almost everyone from the village.

There are less than fifteen men and women still living in Ai's Creek, most of them elderly and people with disabilities, many of them serious. They are like people who failed to escape in time from a disaster. My childhood neighbour Ji Bai has nyctalopia and his vision is extremely poor. His wife died of starvation about sixteen years ago and he then sold his daughter to someone in a remote town so that she might have a better life. These days Ji Bai drives a tricycle, flying over the roads of hardened soil that connect every nearby village and collecting scraps to make a living. The government pays him a subsidy of less than 1,000 yuan per month for transporting rubbish bins in local villages to a waste transfer station. When these fifteen or so people reach the end of their lives, the village will be deserted. Maybe by then the roads will be covered by wildly growing weeds. In fact, some weeds have already grown as tall as small trees. Every village is becoming a ghost village. In order to see this for myself, I walked to four nearby. They are all the same: no longer bustling, they are populated only by the almost-dead who sit quietly on street corners.

The elementary school I went to had only three students and has now closed for good. The construction of the grounds was funded by a company based in a far-away city and there is a well-built basketball court, but the classrooms are now filled with pumpkins and white gourds. People from the city are still concerned about the countryside and those who live there. Goods continue to be donated, hauled to the local villages even while people keep flowing into the city. They move towards and pass each other. The birds and the fish are getting bigger. When I was strolling along the riverbank, a grey bird as big as a rabbit hopped in front of me, startling me terribly.

Countrymen heading to towns and cities are looking for ways to make a living and earn money. At first they are stuck doing cheap labour and some will remain stuck in these roles for the rest of their lives, but many will go on to have decent lives. Of those who left Ai's Creek, the bravest are involved in real-estate development in town and have become the local rich. Their positive spirit of reaching higher and further happens to coincide with the state's plan of accelerating urbanisation.

In the National Plan on New Urbanisation, 2014–2020, issued by the Central Committee of the Communist Party and the State Council in 2014, urbanisation is considered a natural step as society develops. It symbolises the degree of modernity of a country. At the moment, according to the National Plan, the actual urban population is about 53.7 per cent of the total, while the official figure is only around 36 per cent. This number is not only much lower than the 80 per cent average of developed countries, it also does not meet the mean of 60 per cent in developing countries.

I have noticed the change in Ruichang city. What we used to consider rural areas have quietly become towns or cities. Numerous cities in different places (almost everywhere) find themselves in a similar situation, expanding rapidly like monsters. No doubt this expansion will cause conflicts between current landowners and the government, or developers. In the past years, cases of self-immolation and murder associated with housing demolition are not unheard of, all of which are closely related to the National Plan on New Urbanisation. The reason why Ai's Creek remains peaceful is because neither the government nor its inhabitants see any value in the land. Yet I remember that my grandfather used to say, 'You should always own a piece of land, if possible.' Back then, land ownership was a guarantee of survival for farmers. The fate of landless farmers was like duckweed: untied and unpredictable. Now, in the twenty-first century, people's attitudes have changed and in some housing demolition cases, many landowners care more about their compensation than about the land itself.

Justin Jin's photos are realistic depictions of the state of invasive urbanisation in contemporary China. Often the new urban residents dress and behave in a fashion unfitting to modern cities, but in the near future they, or their children, might become a dominating part of those cities. This is what happened with my family. My family is a part of that class: we were born in Ai's Creek, yet everyone now thinks of themselves as a resident of the city, and no one wants to return to the countryside. ■

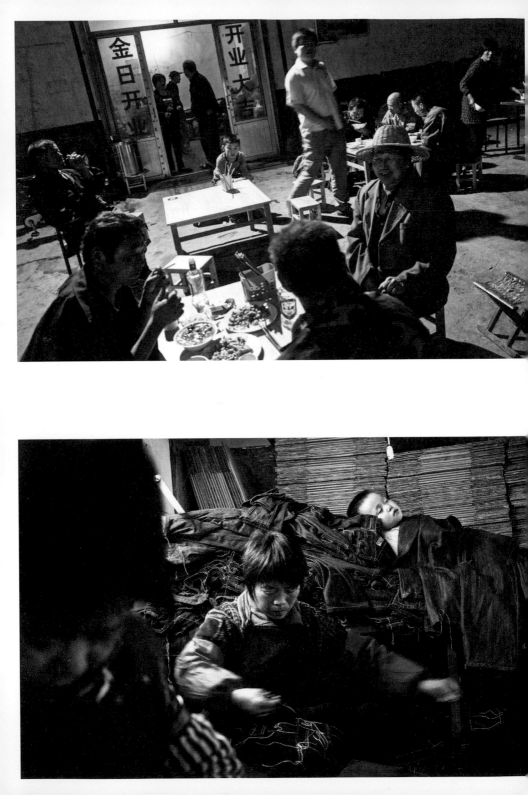

EXPLORE NEW WRITING

Subscribers can now read everything from
this issue and access *Granta*'s entire digital
archive at Granta.com or on the *Granta* app.

PRINT SUBSCRIPTIONS
FROM £32
Includes digital access

DIGITAL-ONLY SUBSCRIPTION
FROM £12

Call + 44(0) 208 955 7011
or complete the subscription form overleaf
or visit granta.com/subscribe

GRANTA

THE MAGAZINE OF NEW WRITING

PRINT SUBSCRIPTION REPLY FORM FOR UK, EUROPE
AND REST OF THE WORLD (includes digital and app access).
For digital-only subscriptions, please visit granta.com/subscriptions.

GUARANTEE: If I am ever dissatisfied with my *Granta* subscription, I will simply notify you, and you will send me a complete refund or credit my credit card, as applicable, for all un-mailed issues.

YOUR DETAILS

TITLE ....

NAME ....

ADDRESS ....

POSTCODE ....

EMAIL ....

☐ Please tick this box if you wish to receive special offers from *Granta*
☐ Please tick this box if you wish to receive offers from organisations selected by *Granta*

YOUR PAYMENT DETAILS

1) ☐ Pay £32 (saving £20) by direct debit.

To pay by direct debit please complete the mandate and return to the address shown below.

2) Pay by cheque or credit/debit card. Please complete below:

1 year subscription: ☐ UK: £36   ☐ Europe: £42   ☐ Rest of World: £46

3 year subscription: ☐ UK: £99   ☐ Europe: £108   ☐ Rest of World: £126

I wish to pay by ☐ CHEQUE   ☐ CREDIT/DEBIT CARD

Cheque enclosed for £_____ made payable to *Granta*.

Please charge £ _____ to my: ☐ Visa ☐ MasterCard ☐ Amex ☐ Switch/Maestro

Card No. ☐☐☐☐☐☐☐☐☐☐☐☐☐☐☐☐

Valid from *(if applicable)* ☐☐ / ☐☐   Expiry Date ☐☐ / ☐☐   Issue No. ☐☐

Security No. ☐☐☐

SIGNATURE .... DATE ....

Instructions to your Bank or Building Society to pay by direct debit

BANK NAME ....

BANK ADDRESS ....

POSTCODE ....

ACCOUNT IN THE NAMES(S) OF: ....

SIGNED .... DATE ....

Bank/building society account number

☐☐☐☐☐☐☐☐

Sort Code

☐☐☐☐☐☐

Originator's Identification

9 1 3 1 3 3

Please mail this order form with payment instructions to:

Granta Publications
12 Addison Avenue
London, W11 4QR
Or call +44(0)208 955 7011 Or visit
GRANTA.COM/SUBSCRIPTIONS for details

Xiaolu Guo in Beijing, 1993
Courtesy of the author

WELL DONE, NO. 3777!

Xiaolu Guo

I grew up in the semi-tropical south, dotted by wet paddy fields, but I always wanted to go to the north, the solemn and tough north. According to the geopolitics of China, the north represents culture and power, while the south retains rotten feudal traditions and trivial domestic comforts. I spent the first nineteen years of my life in the southern Chinese province called Zhejiang, a green hilly region south of Shanghai. There, everything was about agriculture. During the day people toiled in the rice paddies beside their buffaloes; at night three generations ate noodles while listening to the chickens in the backyard.

My mother came from a farmer's family, and my father was a fisherman's son. My father, though, broke with tradition to become a landscape painter – this was very unusual, since our family had been illiterate for generations. Like him, I loved books and art. When I was about fourteen, I began to publish poems in my province's literary magazines. I realised that I wanted to become an artist – and to live in the north. All the great writers and painters I had ever heard of were living in the north. At that time, north in my mind was our great capital Beijing.

I turned eighteen and was about to finish high school. Like other teens in the country, I needed to pass university exams or become a factory worker like my mother. Wearing a heavy pair of glasses, I went to our school library and looked up the name of every college and university in Beijing to try to decide my future. Finally, I decided to apply for film study at the Beijing Film Academy.

Why film? Everyone around me was surprised. Films seemed to belong to a fantasy world. Wanting to enter the film world was like wanting to become an astronaut and fly to the moon. No one in my home town of Wenling had ever met anyone involved in films. My family knew someone who could make porcelain teeth, which was the closest profession to a film-maker we could think of. My decision even startled my father, who believed art was the highest language of human life. Nevertheless, he was supportive of my decision. My mother was suspicious of the direction I was taking. But in my head, one thing was clear: I wanted to be part of the new. And to do that, I needed to study an art that I had no knowledge of or access to.

In the early 1990s, film-making was the most modern art form in the country. I was already seduced by that world. The Russian films dubbed into Chinese that appeared in our cinema – films like *The White Guard*, *Wartime Romance* and *Moscow Does Not Believe in Tears*, were so romantic and heroic that I was convinced that cinema had a much more immediate and direct effect than other art forms. And I could never forget the icy, snowy landscape portrayed in *Doctor Zhivago*, a symbol to me of the great and dramatic revolutionary north.

The task of passing the entrance exams for the film school was an enormous challenge. At that time there was only one film school in China and it was the Beijing Film Academy. You had to physically travel to Beijing and attend a two-week-long exam, which included screenwriting, film history, theatre, vision and sound, as well as general artistic aptitude tests. Although I didn't know anything about the history of cinema, I managed to gather nearly all the books about cinema in the Wenling Library and started to prepare for the exam.

My mother began to get worried. For her, paying my train fare to Beijing, as well as for the hotel, was a waste of money. My father said he would accompany me to the capital, which made it even more expensive. While my parents debated, I was totally consumed by my preparation. One of the annoying aspects of the process was memorising the famous foreign directors' names – like John Ford or Billy Wilder – along with the characteristics of their films. We Chinese translated foreign names phonetically into characters, so John Ford became Yue Han Fu Te – 约翰福特 – and Billy Wilder became Bi Li Wang Er De – 比利怀尔德. My head felt like it was splitting each time I attempted to drive these odd and artificial names into my mind.

When the exam month came, my father and I embarked on the journey to the north. We would have to take an eight-hour bus ride to Hangzhou, the capital city of the province, and from Hangzhou we would take a thirty-six-hour train ride to Beijing. Throughout our cross-country journey, I did not notice anything about the character of the northern landscape that lay outside the window – I was so stressed by the exam that I spent every minute poring over my books.

When we arrived at Beijing Railway Station, we were thrown into a sea of migrants. There were loudspeakers everywhere on the station square, telling us what to do, which only disoriented us further. A voice through one loudspeaker shouted that all passengers should move to exit number 8 to ease the congestion, another told us to queue in the hall until the square was cleared out. For the first time in my life I realised that there were far too many people in China. Achieving anything required a great struggle. You had to fight to even get to the toilet.

For those manic two weeks of the exam period, my father rented us a cheap basement hotel room. It was in the Xinming Hostel – Xinming literally means 'new people', which perfectly summed us up. I wanted to be part of the new, and right here in the capital they had anticipated my desire! The room only cost eight yuan per night, but had no windows or a toilet. All it contained were two hard single beds with sunken pillows and a naked bulb hanging under the damp ceiling. We slept poorly – I had to stuff my ears with toilet paper to block out the coughing and chatting next door.

On the morning of the exam, at six o'clock, my father and I got up. We washed our faces with the freezing cold northern water. By a dusty roadside store next to our hostel, we each ate four hot pork buns, watching the proud Beijing citizens passing us on their bikes, heading to their work units. They looked so solemn and stately, an appearance that the people in my southern home town didn't have. After eating our buns, we wiped our mouths and set off for the film-school campus like soldiers marching to the battlefield.

The campus was crowded with thousands of students with their parents and grandparents. Everybody looked nervous – there was a strained intensity in their body language. We were overwhelmed by the scene. Instantly, I fell into a panic.

At eight o'clock sharp, two exam officers stood up on a ladder poking out from the multitude of bodies and screamed down to the mass: 'Everyone who is participating in the exam will be given a number! Please look for your number on the chalkboard over there!'

The officer pointed, and the mass moved like an oceanic wave towards the supposed chalkboard on the other side of the campus. My father dragged me through the mayhem. Standing on our tiptoes, searching through a great array of numbers and names, we spotted my name and birthdate and found my number: 5001. The total number of candidates was six thousand. I didn't know there would be six thousand students participating in this two-week-long exam for eleven seats each in five departments!

That morning, all six thousand of us were distributed across the campus for the first exam. We had to memorise our numbers and only write those on the exam sheet, as many people had the same name. Parents and family members waited outside as we filed into the exam hall. We were given our exam papers, many sheets of printed paper with questions like: How did the Hollywood film industry rejuvenate its creativity by adopting the methods of European cinema? Give one or two examples to demonstrate your point.

It was a nerve-racking experience, since every night after the day's exam the teachers would narrow down the numbers of participants, announcing those who would proceed to the next stage. Even though everybody was used to our very competitive social system, we were still running like rats through the streets, headless and panicking, every morning. I survived the first three days of the exam. On the fourth day, professors began face-to-face interviews to get a sense of everyone's personality. During one of those sessions, I was told I was out of the game. I had failed the theatre-study exam because I hadn't known who Stanislavsky was, or what method acting meant. So there I was, exiting from the exam room to find my father, who was as disappointed as I was. As the next numbers were called out, a film professor came up to us. He patted me on the shoulder and said to me in very official Mandarin: 'Don't be too sad, 5001, you were doing well with the other subjects. You can come back to try again next year!'

What? Next year! My heart was bursting in pain. I was so hurt by the result that I burst into tears in front of the professor. Didn't he realise how impossible that was? What about all the costs for our hotel, our meals and the train tickets? Who would pay for all those again? My mother would now feel justified in undermining my ambitions completely. Dispirited, my father took me downstairs. Outside the building, we took a last glance at my number – 5001, slightly faded after being up on the chalkboard for four days. On the way back to our New People's Hostel, I saw several students leaving the campus in tears with their grey-faced parents.

But my father wasn't defeated. He instantly took me to a bookshop near the film school and bought a dozen cinema books for me, including a copy of Stanislavsky's biography. 'We will return next year once you finish reading all these books!' my father reassured me. I looked down at the biography and thought, now I have you Konstantin Sergeevich Stanislavsky – you arrogant Russian imperialist! How much I hate you! I swore in my heart that I would soon conquer him. Putting those glossily printed art books into my shoulder bag, I realised how luxurious they were for a provincial kid like me. I felt now that I had a ticket to the film world. Yes, failure is the mother of success.

We were so worn out from the agony of the last weeks that both my father and I slept through the long train journey back to the south. But once we returned to Wenling, my will to conquer the goal had grown even stronger. I spent days and nights studying. My father got his friends to collect any film or theatre books they could find in Wenling – books about Bertolt Brecht and Orson Welles. Although I had never seen these artists' productions, I set myself the task of becoming an 'expert' on their work. I recited the story of each scene from *The Good Woman of Sichuan*, even though I was confused about why a German playwright would write a story set in the province of Sichuan – another place I had never been. Then I memorised the *The Tragedy of Kane: Individualism under Laissez-Faire Capitalism*, a Chinese academic study of Orson Welles's *Citizen Kane*. I even overcame my aversion to Stanislavsky, and drew a connection between method acting and my country's Communist-revolutionary-opera performances. First-hand knowledge was not important for the exam. An unstoppable stream of regurgitated detail would, I hoped, more than satisfy the examiners.

The year passed with my face buried in books. Like a typical Chinese teenager, I never had time to play or be idle. Fun and leisure were remote things in our youth. Our days were filled with compulsory learning and housework – and sometimes labouring on farms or helping in factories after school. Against my mother's will, my father accompanied me again to Beijing when the next set of exams arrived. We stayed in the same hostel. Again, I had no chance to see anything of the capital. There was the same almost unbearable tension of the daily exams, with the results only announced the next day.

During this marathon, I kept seeing my new number, 3777, on the chalkboard for the next round, even though the total number of applicants had increased to seven thousand. In the final interview about screenwriting, one professor asked me what the main difference was between Eastern cinema and Western cinema. I pondered for a second and somehow produced a pithy answer: 'Western cinema is fast and materialistic. Eastern cinema is slow and spiritual.' The professor gaped at me, then his expression softened. His eyebrow rose slightly and he nodded.

When the exams finished, two professors came over to me and said, 'Well done, No. 3777!' My body was stiff, my thoughts racing, I was in the crazed mechanical mode of a frontline soldier, not knowing that the war just ended. We were told to go home and wait for a month until they made their final selection.

When the official letter from the Beijing Film Academy finally arrived at our house, my father was as nervous as I was because he knew this would be my last chance. We could not afford another trip for another exam. If I failed this time I would have to stand at the factory assembly line every day, just like my mother. But when my father finally took the letter from my shaking hands and opened it, he erupted with relief and joy. I had gained one of the eleven places in the Film and Literature Department of Beijing Film Academy. I was in ecstasy.

August of 1993 was the last summer I spent in my sweaty and drowsy southern home province. I could hardly wait. My body was still there, on that heavy brown soil, but my mind had already flown to the moon. In our small kitchen I listened to the news about the world and about Beijing, and felt I was no longer a part of the Wenling mass. No one in this little town gave a damn about the many momentous historical events happening that year. Beijing had just welcomed our new president Jiang Zemin, who had looked very grand on television, although he was much less popular than our previous leader Deng Xiaoping. The people of Wenling hadn't even realised there had been a change of leadership in Beijing.

That same month, the moon had moved to its closest point to Earth in recent history, and thus to the fullest phase of the lunar cycle. Scientists said that the moon appeared to be 30 per cent brighter than any other moon in previous years. One night, my father and I climbed up the bamboo-covered hills behind our house to watch – the brightest moon we had ever seen. It was so large that we could see its shadowy-cratered surface. When we were about to leave, I stood on the hilltop and screamed to the world beneath me: 'Do you see the moon tonight? The moon is much bigger and much brighter than in any other year!' My father laughed. But the world below was oblivious to my announcement. The town of Wenling had been numbed by the throbbing sound of factory machines, traffic, human noise – the mundane activities of daily life.

On the day I left for Beijing, my parents walked me to the bus station. My mother had sewed three hundred yuan into my sweater's inner pocket, and my father was carrying two large bags for me. A long trip lay ahead of me, and this time I would be alone. With mosquitoes biting my skin, my hair knotted and tangled, I grabbed my bags from my father's hands and jumped onto the bus. Then I heard my mother yelling behind me:

'Make sure you eat lamb meat, drink blood soup and chew garlic in Beijing!'

I looked at my mother's face, nodded and hurried to my seat. In the end, I could see my mother was proud of me studying in Beijing. At the very least she cared about some aspects of my future. She knew that I had low blood pressure, and lamb, blood soup and garlic were supposed to be good for a skinny, low-blood-pressure girl like me. My father waved his hands at the bus window and said: 'Write to me!' Yes of course, I said in my heart, I will of course write letters to my father. He was the only person I could write to in this world. No one else. He was the only man I trusted in this world, no other man.

I was nineteen and a half when I left my southern home town for the big city. During that three-day journey to the capital, I stared at the mountains and rivers outside the window. It was the first time I really used my eyes to see my country, and I felt like writing a long epic poem as the train rushed along. The scenery slowly evolved from the poetic south to the utilitarian north. In 1993, China was an enormous construction site, full of grey industrial foundations and factories. But it still looked beautiful to me.

In the early dawn, the train crossed the Yangtze River and came into Nanjing. I got up from my seat, stretched my neck and looked down at the muddy yellow water. This was the Yangtze, the longest river in Asia, the great border between northern and southern China, and the very river Chairman Mao had often swum across during his lifetime. The chairman knew well that to build his strength he had to undertake physical challenges. He was a swimmer, and the Yangtze River was the most famous body of water in China. But it was also a river flowing with a thousand legends to the East China Sea. My heart cried out: 'I have made it! Heaven and Hell, I have managed to leave my backwater for civilisation. I can finally live alone and live freely, in the great north!'

In Beijing, I swallowed kilos of lamb, blood tofu and garlic. I took my parents' words to heart. I felt strong. I studied hard. I wanted to become someone big, to belong in the big capital of a big country. I didn't miss Wenling, even though I often dreamed on my dormitory bed of walking through the bamboo forests in my province, trying to find the fishpond where we children had always played. In my dream, the laughter from the kids was loud and vivid, the bamboo forest shimmering in the steaming summer air. I've never encountered that landscape again. ∎

ON THE ROAD

Janine di Giovanni

At Cedar Rapids airport I found a place to plug in my iPhone –
a lifeline to the world I leave behind too often – and a corner
table someone had just abandoned. The waitress, unsmiling, tattooed,
dark roots with frosted blonde hair, took my order. She came back
in no time at all with a scorching plate of microwaved nachos and
half a gallon of Diet Coke in a plastic cup. I burned my fingers on
the plate.

I had been on the road for two weeks and I was bone tired.
I missed my son, I missed my own bed with clean white sheets,
I missed my home. I missed making coffee in the morning in my glass
pot and looking out at the early-morning light, purple in winter, pink
in summer, over Boulevard Raspail.

This journey had been relatively painless – no wars, no conflicts
– but I had moved every few days from Airbnbs to hotels with
cardboard-like beds and lukewarm showers and insomnia at 3 a.m.
with no pills to drive me into sleep.

At the start of autumn, with the leaves beginning to change and the
air growing cooler, I had set off on an American odyssey. It began in
New York, moved to Frenchtown, New Jersey, then Detroit and Iowa
City, where long ago I had been an awkward young graduate student

in the Iowa Writers' Workshop. I had applied because my literary heroes had been students and teachers there – Flannery O'Connor, Raymond Carver, Tennessee Williams, Marilynne Robinson, Robert Lowell – and I wanted to become a writer, too.

I had come back to Iowa City to teach, but by the time I arrived at Cedar Rapids airport I was spent. In the weeks before my American odyssey, I had driven from Erbil in northern Iraq to Dohuk and then to Mount Sinjar to live with female Yazidi soldiers fighting ISIS. I had slept on a rooftop with fighters who woke at 6 a.m. with the fierce Iraqi sun to do military exercises. On the way home, I stopped in Lalesh, the Yazidi spiritual home, and villages close to Mosul.

The months before that had been a blur of airports and hotels: Stockholm, Oslo, Athens, Istanbul, Brussels, Oslo again, London, Dublin, New York, Paris and, finally, my mother's home in Red Bank, New Jersey. While I was lying in those unfamiliar beds, I was running through my next trips: Berlin, Frankfurt, Los Angeles, New York again, then Spain, Damascus, Aleppo, Geneva, Gaziantep, Istanbul, New York again, and in the new year Australia, India and Davos.

The irony and the juxtaposition of the places does not escape me: Davos and Aleppo, for example. I wish I could take in more of each place when I am there. I also wish I was with loved ones and not alone when I hear momentous game-changing news, such as the Brexit vote or Donald Trump's election, both of which I learned waking up in strange hotels. I had no one to share my horror with but the waiter who served me coffee. It made me feel that I was walking through history in a steady but solitary line.

I must not complain. These days, travel is much easier than it was when I rocked up in Grozny or Sarajevo for months and months with no return ticket, a sleeping bag and a few hundred-dollar bills. In East Timor, I slept on a piece of wood that had been a doorframe, for a month, with no complaints and no back pain. In Sarajevo, I lived for years in a room with plastic-covered windows, and ate breakfast, lunch and dinner from tinned goods in humanitarian aid boxes.

Now I get hotels (sometimes very nice ones; sometimes the Iowa House with the cardboard bed) and taxis to and from the airport. No more hitchhiking to the Gaza Strip as I once did, aged twenty-six. Now I have Uber, LeCab, Juno; Air France and RATP apps on my phone; WhatsApp; Telegram and Apple Pay. Conveniences.

But I still get homesick, that vast and deep pit in the stomach, every time I go away. In Iowa City, as I returned to my 25-year-old self, I tried to marvel at the iron bridge built by FDR as part of his New Deal policy in 1936 as it hung over the flooding river. I liked waking up early and walking to breakfast at the Bluebird Diner where I could get blueberry pancakes – something I can't always find in Paris. The wideness, the brashness of the Midwestern sky made me happy – the freshness of it, the simple beauty. I am happy to speak English and not think in a foreign language, and to see the ease and uncomplicated grace of large blond wheat-fed American kids in sweatshirts and sneakers.

I have been homesick as long as I can remember: from the time I left my parents' house, aged seventeen, and never really returned home again, other than for holidays. My sense of isolation started early, even when I was part of a larger family, albeit an outsider from the start. I remember being six and, unable to sleep, knocking on the wall that separated my room from that of my two brothers'. There was an exquisite joy in hearing the muffled knock back from one or the other sibling, and realising I was not alone in the night.

Many years later I read Proust and found that he, too, suffered from that nocturnal misery. Sick, alone in a hotel, he saw a crack of light under the door and felt his heart quicken with relief – it was morning and servants would be rising to make the tea and start a new day.

But no, he found, a few minutes later, that the crack of light was an electric lamp that someone had left on. Then they turned it off. Such pain and loneliness in being sick and alone.

M y old childhood room is gone. My brothers who slept next to me and knocked on the wall died very young, both tragically. I cannot think of them as young boys with fishing rods and cans of live bait without feeling my throat close with sorrow. The house where my father had planted trees, one for each of his seven children, was sold decades ago, and all of our ghostly footsteps on the stairs in the front hall, I imagine, are silenced.

My tree was a cherry blossom that flowered, bloomed and eventually fell to the ground. My brothers had chestnut trees, weeping willows, hydrangeas.

I am not old, not even middle-aged, but still I sometimes try to remember all of my telephone numbers going back to childhood, and I always miss a few: what was my phone number when I lived in Maine? When I lived in London?

In Iowa City, I went for a long walk past the house where I had lived with my first love, my first husband, and tried to find the front porch where we had sat drinking beer. Our neighbors included a manic-depressive who sometimes forgot to take his lithium and ran circles in the parking lot, and a pretty triathlete named Helen, nicknamed Bion (short for Bionic), who owned a tarantula. The house was on a dangerous corner of Iowa Avenue, and our running joke was that a big Saturday night was waiting on the front porch for a traffic accident, as nothing much ever happened in Iowa City. So I left, moved to England and began a life in motion.

Traveling is easier now. It's faster. You check in, you check out. You go to an airport and board a plane with something on your telephone. You get Wi-Fi in the skies. You keep photos on your iPhone to remind you of home. We can FaceTime our children, our loved ones, and we can see them in living color – their imperfections, their crooked teeth, their anger. Their secrets grow deeper the longer we are away.

And when you get back, you unpack. You sit on the bed and sort through piles and piles of bills. You feed the cat, kiss your offspring, telephone those you love but always leave behind. You begin the cycle again, and suddenly you realize you are home – but you are still homesick. ■

What is travel writing? One of this magazine's former editors, Bill Buford, described it as 'pre-eminently a narrative told in the first person, authenticated by lived experience' – a definition that appeared in *Granta*'s travel issue of 1984, around the time that the genre reached the height of its post-war literary fashion. Bill might have added that the narrative usually finds its focus in a journey, though not necessarily a long journey. Apsley Cherry-Garrard travelled nearly to the South Pole; George Orwell went to Lancashire. The memorable books that came out of their travels, *The Worst Journey in the World* and *The Road to Wigan Pier*, have their origins in different impulses; when Cherry-Garrard set out with Captain Scott a book was the last thing on his mind – it was the expedition's disaster that impelled him to write one – whereas Orwell set out for Wigan with a publisher's contract in his pocket and an ambition to describe the travails of the working class. He knew he went to write a book, and always had an eye for material; Cherry-Garrard's account, on the other hand, could be seen merely as a literary by-product of a grander calling. The difference lies between travelling to write and travelling for some other purpose (warfare, exploration, scientific discovery, pure adventure) and then writing about it – or not; only in the twentieth century did writers begin to see travel writing as a self-financing literary form.

A remarkable number of them have been English or England-domiciled: Patrick Leigh Fermor, V.S. Naipaul, Norman Lewis, Eric Newby, Jonathan Raban, Bruce Chatwin, Colin Thubron, Bill Bryson, Paul Theroux. One of the most influential (and unreliable), Ryszard Kapuściński, came from Poland. Only a few have been women: from England, they include Freya Stark, Emily Eden and Jan (formerly

James) Morris, and from Ireland, Dervla Murphy. Like many of my generation, I owe a lot of what passes as my understanding of the world to these names – they made me interested to see the places they described and gave me at least a glimmer of an insight into their history and way of living. They also gave me days and weeks of amusement. Travel writing at some elementary level amounts to the exploitation of difference – comic misunderstanding is part of the traveller's tradition and people and things that are both different and far away, socially or geographically, are tempting targets for the humorist. Colonialism and feelings of Western superiority have played a part in this – the critic Jonathan Keates described one school of travel writing as 'Old Etonian on a bicycle' – but then travel writing of most kinds, not just the humorous, has the history of colonialism perched on its shoulder.

Outside the trenches of the ocean deep, none of the physical world remains to be explored. Thirty years on from the travel-writing boom of the 1980s, new technologies have made the globe smaller, quicker, and, at least superficially, many times more knowable. The balance of power within it has shifted from West to East. A traveller on the plane from London to Delhi or Shanghai knows he is flying into the future and leaving the past behind. The assurance that was part of the travel writer's equipment – the unspoken notion that where he came from was richer, safer and more modern than the place he found himself – has withered; the Western traveller's jaunty superiority is almost dead and the days of cavalier travel writing – India on Monday, Burma on Tuesday – are over.

*

New ways have been found to tell us about abroad and at their best give us a profounder understanding of it. A few years ago, the American reporter Katherine Boo spent many months living in a Mumbai slum to produce her book *Behind the Beautiful Forevers*, with its insights into the complexity of poor lives. Twenty years before, V.S. Naipaul had found the slum too daunting to enter (he records the experience in *India: A Million Mutinies Now*). Which is the travel writer? Neither, probably, would want to be known as one, but, by excluding herself from the book's narrative, it's Boo who discards the age-old stance of the travel account: the curious outsider.

That standpoint isn't without its uses. It could be enlightening, for example, to read modern accounts of travels in the Western world by writers from the East; if nothing else, we might then know how it feels to be ironised, condescended to and found morally wanting. Several such books may be in the offing. Some of our own medicine is surely coming our way.

Travel writing isn't dead. It just isn't what it was. ■

When I look at my vast and growing collection of literary works about faraway places it seems as though I have been obsessed with travel writing for a long time. In my imagination I have been to many villages and cities in the world; crawled up to a hut on top of a mountain; heard winds of the desert singing – my quest to know other people and lands never ends.

I suspect that much of my own mental travelling had its genesis in my cultural background. To Aboriginal people of Australia, the land itself holds a vast archive of ancestral travel through a spiritual landscape. These are the stories in the library of my mind, and where I am travelling in the books I have read about our country. Did I need to do so much reading about other places? Yes – if only to discover small miracles of thought imagined elsewhere, which helps me get closer to the truth of my home.

Reading travel writing is part of my endless search to get closer to the world – even if just as a poor visitor trying to look through the cracks of other people's culture. It has enriched my imagination as I travel my own culture, either through the mind or on journeys through traditional country – the only kind of travel the vast majority of Aboriginal people ever do. Or travelling to too many funerals – we are funeral tourists, many of our people now say. This realisation, the consequence of historic and continuing government policy control and failure, has become a new part of an old story about what happens when the narratives of our world are kidnapped and distorted, or deliberately muted or silenced and controlled by the powerful narratives of interests outside of the Aboriginal world.

While my library contains the works of travel writers, I have mostly searched for those who speak about their own place in the world. But the world is changing and many people have no place to call home.

Some of the most important kinds of travel writing now are stories of flight, written by people who belong to the millions of asylum seekers in the world. These are stories that are almost too hard to tell, but which, once read, will never be forgotten. Some of these stories had to be smuggled out of detention centres, or were caught covertly on smuggled mobiles in snatches of calls on weak connections from remote and distant prisons. Why is this writing important? Behrouz Boochani, a Kurdish journalist and human rights campaigner who has been detained on Manus Island for over three years with no hope for release yet in sight, puts it plainly in a message to the world in the anthology *Behind the Wire*. It is, he wrote, 'because we need to change our imagination'. ■

The death of travel – and of the travel book – has been predicted for almost a century. Writers as diverse as Joseph Conrad, Evelyn Waugh and Claude Lévi-Strauss long ago decided that travel writing, and travel itself, was finished. Nowadays, runs the obituary, the world has become overpopulated, and has grown too familiar through the ease of air flight and the computer screen.

There is a supposition, too, that travel writing is a postcolonial presumption: a notion that reduces all contact between 'First World' and 'Third World' cultures to a patronising act of acquisition. No mention here of travel as an avenue of understanding, of self-education or of empathy. Any meeting between unequal worlds is seen in terms of dominance – a notion that threatens to turn all human contact into paranoia.

In fact the travel-writing genre is infinitely resilient and varied. Just as the world itself changes, so the priorities and sensibilities of those who write and travel it change too. The old patrician stress on the historical and aesthetic, with its assumption of a shared culture between writer and reader, has loosened into more personal and demotic writing, whose locus may not be the Acropolis but the coffee shop beneath it. So the baton passes down from Paul Theroux and Dervla Murphy to Rory MacLean, Sara Wheeler and Philip Marsden, and on to Oliver Bullough, Tim Butcher and many others – and the sheer variety of interest and enterprise defies prediction.

A more insidious threat to individual travel is the notion that the world is too much known, readily experienced at the touch of a keypad. But this too is an illusion. Just as one country opens up, the curtain comes down on another. Fifty years ago huge swathes of Asia – two thousand miles eastward as the crow flies, from Damascus through Afghanistan to Peshawar – could be traversed easily by car, while the old Soviet Union and China – now accessible – were largely off limits.

Whatever the current state of travel writing (which reached its popular peak in the 1980s) its continuance over the centuries belies its death sentence. No computer can substitute for experience on the ground, the traveller's raw intimacy with the sensuous texture of a place: its smells and tastes, its street life and conversations. Nothing can equal the deracination from a person's own culture and exposure to another. Once immersed in a self-chosen journey (the difference, here, between the traveller and the tourist) you feel that the world has expanded and grown diverse again, because it is no longer familiar, and you are travelling not by Google, or by air, but by local bus or train or perhaps – wonderfully – on foot. ■

E xactly forty years ago, modern travel writing had its *annus mirabilis*. Patrick Leigh Fermor published *A Time of Gifts*, the opening book of his now-classic trilogy about walking from the Hook of Holland to Constantinople; Bruce Chatwin published his first and best book, *In Patagonia*; and John McPhee published *Coming into the Country*, his landmark exploration of Alaska and its communities. Another exceptional book, very different to the other three, not least in that it was by a woman, also appeared in 1977 – but for the moment I will leave it unnamed.

It is no accident that the late 1970s should have seen such a surge of travel-writing excellence. These books all arrived towards the end of a decade in which international air travel had become widely affordable, and in which globalisation had begun to standardise even far-flung places. Such developments posed serious challenges for travel writing in what might be called its late-imperial mode, whereby the discovery of terra incognita was the default aim, and the heroic male adventurer the default protagonist. How was the 'other' to be encountered when the world was homogenising so rapidly? How was valour to be performed upon such a crowded stage? Susan Sontag diagnosed the problem as terminal in 1984, declaring travel writing to have become a 'literature of disappointment', unable – like the empires that had chiefly whelped it – to come to terms with its dwindling demesne and diminished responsibilities. Sontag was wrong, though. The crisis of territory didn't hobble travel writing – it revolutionised it. The best writers rose to the challenge by seeking not originality of destination, but originality of form.

Certainly, Chatwin, McPhee and Leigh Fermor could hardly have been more contrasting as stylists. This is Leigh Fermor describing a sunset:

The flatness of the Alföld leaves a stage for cloud-events at sunset that are dangerous to describe: levitated armies in deadlock and riderless squadrons descending in slow motion to smouldering and sulphurous lagoons where barbicans gradually collapse and fleets of burning triremes turn dark before sinking.

This is Bruce Chatwin describing a sunset:

In a brick-red sunset I came to the cottage of a German. He lived with a scrawny Indian boy.

And this is John McPhee describing a sunset:

The air was cool now, nearing fifty . . . We sat around the campfire for at least another hour. We talked of rain and kestrels, oil and antlers, the height and the headwaters of the river. In the night the air and the river balanced out, and both were forty-six at seven in the morning.

Fermor's sunset is epic, reflexive, an event of style, a sentence which burns itself magnificently down in honour of the day's own inferno. He knows the risks he is taking with his tone (the cloud-events are 'dangerous to describe') but writes with the confidence of a hyperbolist good enough to earn his excess: meteorology-as-battle, the gradual combustions, the Germanic delay of that last vital verb until, at last, it is reached and the whole scene subsides to its close.

Chatwin's sunset is sparse, incidental – atmospheric in a literal sense. It is a caption, really, written by a man who had worked as caption writer and cataloguist at Sotheby's. Chatwin's prose has often been celebrated for its clarity, and he achieved this clarity by subtraction, where Leigh Fermor achieved his moods by multiplication. 'It's very good,' Leigh Fermor told Chatwin's wife Elizabeth, of *In Patagonia*, 'but he ought to let himself rip.' 'It's very good,' Chatwin told Elizabeth of *A Time of Gifts*, 'but it's too baroque and overflowing; he should tone it down.'

Then there is McPhee's sunset – in which the sun doesn't feature at all, eclipsed from the scene as it is by facts. McPhee's prose here concerns balance, and is balanced: note how carefully those three pairs of nouns match each other (singular noun, plural noun; rain, oil, height; kestrels, antlers, headwaters), preparing for the equalised temperature relationship of air and river at exactly 'seven in the morning'. McPhee – a *New Yorker* staff writer for more than half a century – is a man committed to accuracy and to metrics. *Coming into the Country*, like his other books, carries an astonishing density of detail: his non-fiction, as David Remnick has observed, emulates the 'freedom' of fiction but not its 'licence'.

All three of these books hot-wired the neo-Victorian travelogue. *In Patagonia* was puckish, unreliable, dazzlingly experimental in its mosaic form, and a sly burlesque of the colonial quest-narrative: Chatwin sets off in search of a piece of brontosaurus skin, and ends up finding sloth turds on a cave floor at the end of the world. *A Time of Gifts* was by turns a baroque adventure in historiography, an interrogation of the nature of memory, and a heartbreaking tour through the since-shattered world of 1930s Mitteleuropa. *Coming into the Country* was an intricately patterned enquiry into America's relationship with the idea of wilderness, braced by an awesome integrity of observation.

The legacies of these three books are with us still, in terms of the ripostes they offered to the notion that travel writing was dependent on novelty of territory rather than novelty of address. Among those many writers influenced by Chatwin was W.G. Sebald, who in turn became a vastly significant figure in the tradition. 'Just as Chatwin himself ultimately remains an enigma,' Sebald remarked in a short but fascinating essay on Chatwin, published a year before Sebald's untimely death in 2001:

> One never knows how to classify his books. All that is obvious is that their structure and intentions place them in no known genre. Inspired by a kind of avidity for the undiscovered, they move along a line where the points of demarcation are those strange manifestations and objects of which one cannot say whether they are among the phantasms generated in our minds from time immemorial.

Sebald might, of course, have been writing about his own unclassifiable 'prose fictions' here: haunted as they are by phantasms who could be archetypes, polymorphous as they are in form, and travelling as they do widely in time though not broadly in space. The 'undiscovered' country in Chatwin's work, as in Sebald's, is largely a shadowed realm of the mind.

In the forty years since 1977, so many of the most brilliant writers of travel and place have – like Chatwin, McPhee and Leigh Fermor – sought to forge new forms and styles appropriate to their subjects, and to allow a bleeding-together of mental and actual terrain. I think here, in addition to Sebald, of William Least Heat-Moon's 'deep maps' of America; of Pico Iyer's cracklingly hyper-connective global tours; of Iain Sinclair's psychogeographic *dérives* and Václav Cílek's psychogeological essays; of Rebecca Solnit's fierce fusions of politics, memory and landscape; of the books of Sara Wheeler, Nicholas Rothwell, William Dalrymple, Redmond O'Hanlon, Geoff Dyer, Colin Thubron and Jan Morris; and of a young Indian writer called Simar Kaur, who lives in the Indian Himalayas, where she is writing a remarkable first book – poised somewhere between ethnography and experimental fiction – called *The Sky Road*, about the truckers of the Leh–Manali Highway. Meanwhile, the scale and structure of the Anthropocene charges travel literature with new obligations and confronts it with new crises: how to represent the dispersed consequences of climate change and mass extinction, for instance, or how to map and track the so-called 'hyperobjects' with which we are so entangled.

What, though, of the fourth great travel book of 1977, the one I left unnamed? That was *The Living Mountain*, by Anna 'Nan' Shepherd – and how dissimilar it was to its three famous peers. The others were published, to fanfares of press and praise, by major trade publishing houses; Shepherd's slipped out in a tiny print run from Aberdeen University Press, with scarcely a review to its name. The other three were written by men; Shepherd's was explicitly, though not exclusively, about what it meant to be a woman walking alone in wild country. The other three were all variously animated by ideas of remoteness; Shepherd confined herself to a single nearby region, the Cairngorm massif in north-east Scotland.

Yet Shepherd's book has been at least as influential as Chatwin's, McPhee's or Leigh Fermor's. It is one of the works – J.A. Baker's *The Peregrine* (1967) is another – that has inspired and energised the recent British renaissance of landscape writing. It has found its way into the work of countless artists, musicians, poets, photographers and calligraphers in Britain and beyond. Shepherd's importance to the culture of what she calls her 'dark and stubborn country' of Scotland was recognised by the Royal Bank of Scotland's decision to feature her words and image on its new £5 note, first issued in September 2016.

For *The Living Mountain* is about the Cairngorms in the same way that *Moby-Dick* is about whaling ships or *Mrs Dalloway* about London streets. It vibrates dazzlingly between the specific and the universal, and between matter and metaphysics. Shepherd describes what she calls 'the total mountain', a holistic account of the massif in which human presence, creaturely life, elements and weather are coextensive. She does so in prose that is deeply wise, avidly sensual and, we might say, committed to uncertainty. 'Slowly I have found my way in,' she writes of the Cairngorms, but 'if I had other senses there are other things I should know'. Always, in Shepherd, movement across landscape has its corresponding inward journey, and place is somewhere we are in and not on.

Here she is, describing a winter Cairngorm sunset:

> The intense frost, the cloudless sky, the white world, the setting sun and the rising moon, as we gazed on them from the slope of Morrone, melted into a prismatic radiation of blue, yellow, mauve and rose. The full moon floated up into green light; and as the rose and violet hues spread over snow and sky, the colour seemed to live its own life, to have body and resilience, as though we were not looking at it, but were inside its substance. ∎

RE-ENTRY

Andrew McConnell

Introduction by Adam Marek

When NASA retired its space shuttle fleet in 2011, the job of commuting astronauts to and from the International Space Station returned to the birthplace of human spaceflight: the Baikonur Cosmodrome in Kazakhstan. It was from here, in 1961, that the Vostok spacecraft rocketed Yuri Gagarin 169 kilometres up, out of our atmosphere, to perform a single loop of the Earth. The vehicles that ferry today's star-sailors look like they come from the same era.

The Soyuz capsule has been Russia's cosmic workhorse for fifty years now. While it's had a number of refinements over the decades, its design remains outwardly similar. It's old-school space travel, but if you want to travel to the ISS, the Soyuz is your only option right now.

When you come back to Earth in a Soyuz, you fall to Earth. The whole return journey from the ISS to the Kazakh Steppe takes 3.5 hours, the final thirty minutes of which are a terrifying plummet, the three astronauts cramped inside experiencing 4G, hurtling towards the planet at 2,800 kilometres per hour. As they punch through the atmosphere, the capsule becomes a fireball. Everything shakes. Sparks fly past the window. At 30,000 feet, the first of a series of parachutes opens, slowing the Soyuz's descent, until 70 cm above the ground, retrorockets fire to slow it further, and it strikes the ground with a thump.

Russian cosmonauts refer to the moment of returning to Earth and emerging from the charred capsule as a 'second birth'. After months on the space station, their muscles have atrophied and they are baby-weak. Initially, they cannot walk by themselves. They are pulled from the pod by the ground crew.

'I wanted to see a human's expression after returning from space,' photographer Andrew McConnell says. 'I knew there was something magical in this.'

Look at the picture of the astronaut smelling a flower on page 108. This is Samantha Cristoforetti. See the expression on her face; she has just spent 199 days cramped in an orbital tour bus, setting the record for the longest single space flight by a female astronaut. Cristoforetti returned in June 2015, to a steppe in full bloom. From her chair, she pointed to a flower and one of the ground crew picked it for her. 'When she smelled it,' Andrew says, 'Her face lit up.'

In McConnell's photos, two worlds collide. The Soyuz capsule – an apogee of human ingenuity and endeavour – meets the Kazakh Steppe, where daily routines are dictated by the passing of the seasons. People here know how to catch fish and shoot ducks. What better place to be reacquainted with the Earth than this wilderness?

This moment in time that McConnell has captured is vanishing. 'Soon,' he says, 'these pictures will look nostalgic.' NASA has selected Boeing and SpaceX to start transporting astronauts to and from the ISS from the end of 2017. Their use of Russian Soyuz capsules will almost certainly be phased out soon after that. And then we'll enter a new age of human space flight. We'll leave behind the era of grey cockpits bristling with switches and enter Elon Musk's gleaming touchscreen wonderland, where space travel will once again look futuristic. ∎

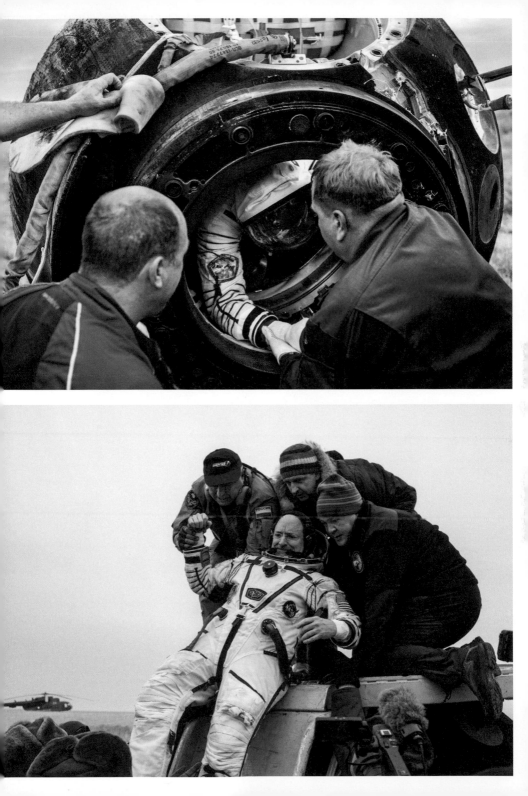

GRANTA

THE MAGAZINE OF NEW WRITING

PRINT SUBSCRIPTION REPLY FORM FOR US, CANADA
AND LATIN AMERICA (includes digital and app access).
For digital-only subscriptions, please visit granta.com/subscriptions.

GUARANTEE: If I am ever dissatisfied with my *Granta* subscription, I will simply notify you, and you will send me a complete refund or credit my credit card, as applicable, for all un-mailed issues.

YOUR DETAILS

TITLE ....

NAME ....

ADDRESS ....

....

CITY.. STATE ....

ZIP CODE .... COUNTRY................................

EMAIL ....

☐ Please tick this box if you wish to receive special offers from *Granta*
☐ Please tick this box if you wish to receive offers from organisations selected by *Granta*

PAYMENT DETAILS

1 year subscription: ☐ US: $48   ☐ Canada: $56   ☐ Latin America: $68

3 year subscription: ☐ US: $120   ☐ Canada: $144   ☐ Latin America: $180

Enclosed is my check for $ ——————— made payable to *Granta*.

Please charge my: ☐ Visa   ☐ MasterCard   ☐ Amex

Card No. ☐☐☐☐☐☐☐☐☐☐☐☐☐☐☐☐

Expiration date ☐☐ / ☐☐

Security Code ☐☐☐☐☐

SIGNATURE .... DATE ....

Please mail this order form with your payment instructions to:

Granta Publications
PO Box 359
Congers, NY 10920-0359

Or call 845-267-3031
Or visit GRANTA.COM/SUBSCRIPTIONS for details

Source code: BUS138PM

CHEKHOV'S LADIES

Edna O'Brien

Malachi *is brushing her hair, long, dark brown and with russet glints. She likes it, as he can tell from her smile in the mirror. It is Bathsheba. As he brushes, the hair takes on an added lustre, sparks of electricity emanating from every single rib, which recklessly he nibbles. He barely knows her, so how can he be brushing her hair.*

He wakens with a jolt and sees the range of mauve mountain through the aeroplane window, misted over, as he has so often sighted them on his regular journeys to and from Dublin. The watchful mountain. How he wishes that he were not going home just then, that he could go elsewhere, to steady himself and forget the beguilements of Manhattan. He signals the hostess to bring him another whiskey, though the bar is shut and she disappears, returning instantly and placing a miniature in the palm of his hand. He has had a few since they set out from New York, but intends to sober up at the airport with coffee, and take gulps of air before the drive home, navigating the corkscrew bends. Showers, stray sheep, bushes warped from wind and a few skeleton trees, effigies to a shorn world.

During his six days in New York everything centred on *Uncle Vanya*, Chekhov's play, which he had transplanted to Ireland and for which there was a workshop in a loft somewhere in SoHo. It was hoped that there might be a production in Providence, Rhode Island, sometime in the autumn. Rhode Island, same name as his wife's hens, lazying in their dust baths in the summer days.

The company showered him with welcome, a rocking chair no less, Barry's Gold label tea and a samovar in salutation to their hero, Anton Chekhov. He felt reborn as a writer, after so many years of stagnancy and botched attempts. He was forty-four, exactly the same age as when Chekhov retched into a spittoon, before he drank the legendary glass of champagne and died. They were curious to know why he had transposed the play to Ireland and he said there were similarities in Russian literature, what with run-down estates, crumbling houses, melancholia and madness. At this, Bathsheba smiled. An odalisque in Turkish trousers, the ochre material bunched around her thin ankles, her eyes were dark, deep-set and burnt with a fierceness. She alternated the parts of Sonya and Elena and in both she was electrifying, the besotted, suffering Sonya and the brittle, capricious Elena. She lived in Brooklyn and had a cat. Her ancestors, as she told them, were from Vladivostok, but forcibly emigrated to China and in her possession was an embroidered silk shawl that had belonged to her mother's mother, Olga. This mother's mother, having been tortured in a camp in Japan, to which they were later despatched, had chosen to endure her punishment as if caught in the throes of religious ecstasy, and died confounding her torturers. One of Bathsheba's earliest memories was of Christmas in some distant country, being fed potato stuffing from a spoon, except that the spoon was too wide and unwieldy for her mouth. Fragments and yet enough for him to conceive of a whole history. Surprising them one day, she did a headstand to beguile poor besotted Uncle Vanya and multiple needles fell from her hair. They were, as she explained, from when she had gone to her acupuncturist, a Dr Wong in Brooklyn. Was Dr Wong also enmeshed in those thickets of hair?

When the director encouraged Malachi to tell them something of his own life, he hesitated, not wanting to describe the everyday routine, incessant rain, walking Nestor, his red setter, morning and evening, closeting himself in his study for hours on end and his first whiskey at six, regardless of when clocks changed. He did not mention the recent film festival in the local school and how he and Oonagh had seen some great Italian films, both of them falling for the waif enchantments of Giulietta Masina in *La Strada* and walking home holding hands, invigorated.

'There is a story I never wrote,' he began and they sat on the floor in a circle, quiet, intent, and even the actress who was playing the old nurse in *Vanya* put her precious knitting aside. He recalled a summer's day when he set out in search of a story that had puzzled him for many years. It was about twenty miles away, in a district called Ballindubh, so named because the branches of the trees on either side of the road had met and meshed, and in summer it was like a glade under there. The story was of two warring brothers, ending in two gruesome deaths. Feargal, their groom and factotum, was the only person who knew it inside out and knew the motives, but had always kept his silence. Feargal lived in the tiny gate lodge at the entrance to the back avenue and was known to be contrary.

Malachi painted a picture of that scorching day, his knocking on the cottage door and Feargal calling *I'm on the lavatory*, while a dog barked crazily to be let out. He waited in the yard and watched the midges swarm in off the lake, the water with its dazzling brightness, the yard all neglect, full of weeds, thistles and old defunct machinery, including two vintage cars, mounted on blocks of wood and cement. There was a rhubarb bed in one corner, the big crinkled leaves sweating in the sun. Then Feargal appeared, tying a bit of rope around his trousers, all talk and twinkle. *Fine, the finest* he said and put his rude good health down to a cup of buttermilk and raw herring every day. Yes, the pheasants were thinning out and the woodcock not right since that disaster over in Chernobyl. By the way he kept talking and shifting, it was clear, as Malachi told them, that he guessed the reason for the visit – *a penman with a notebook, snooping for scandal*. The small dog, Biscuit, was going insane at the advent of a visitor, so much so that Feargal held her upside down, as he might an old mat, then flung her into one of the motor cars, where she perched on a pile of old newspapers. Once installed, she performed little ballets, as with one paw and then the other, she tapped upon the windscreen. If she were let loose, said Feargal, she would run under the hole in the hedge, head off and get stolen or shot. The countryside, he insisted, was gone to rot, hippies flooding in, thieves, robbers and sharks grabbing sites with water frontage, for half nothing. The bastard developer, his neighbour, had bought the Glebe for a song. It lay empty for years, covered in briars, yet yer man spotted it and was now lord of the manor, even stopped him from bringing home a creel of turf. The problem was an adjoining right of way, a little track that the brothers had given him, except that he had no piece of paper to prove it. *I was a right mug* he kept saying and recalled the name of a solicitor that he should have consulted at the time. The two brothers, Michael Patrick and Michael John, were known to be inseparable, always seen at Mass together and at race meetings and were horse-mad. On the eve of a big race in County Limerick, Michael Patrick's horse Rubicon, who was favourite with the bookmakers, staggered as she was led out the stable door, froth spilling from her mouth and within minutes, she collapsed on the cobbles. The investigations that followed were massive, Guards going from house to house and suspicion falling on this person or that. About three months later, the parish priest received an anonymous letter, saying that the writer knew beyond any doubt that the culprit was none other than Michael John, who had been procuring strychnine illegally from chemists in different parishes, saying his lands and his yards were plagued with foxes. From that day on the brothers were at war and never spoke again. Everything in the house was halved and Mrs Boyce, who did the weekly washing, described how cups, saucers, saucepans and cutlery were all divided up. In the big cold hall, with stuffed pine martens in glass cases, a line of blue rope separated each brother's quarters and each kept to his own staircase, when they came or went to fetch grub from the kitchen. On the anniversary of the fatality, as dusk fell, Michael Patrick stood on the top step of his staircase waiting for his brother to appear, then aimed his shotgun, firing several times.

Immediately afterwards he got into his car and drove five miles up the road to a slate quarry, where he took his own life by putting a revolver in his mouth. Locals were shocked at how gruesome it was, how inhuman, brothers who had been bosom friends yielding to such barbarity. Was it the loss of the horse they wondered, or perhaps as young men both had courted the same woman on separate nights in the woods, or maybe the overweening attachment to Mother, whom they always referred to as *Mammy*.

'I could see I was getting nowhere with the real story,' Malachi told his listeners and enacted how suddenly Feargal had changed tactics, all umbrage, saying he hadn't had his first cup of tea, then hurrying into his cottage and slamming the door.

He described the strange aftermath, his walking up the road to where his car was parked and Feargal running after him, calling his name, then, as they came face-to-face, handing him an armful of rhubarb, saying that since his poor wife died, he had no use for it. *It might be in bed at night, that I'd think of them long ago things you're after, but they're gone and they're better gone* Feargal said and at that he ran across the fields singing some raucous song, joyously.

'So I never wrote it,' Malachi said.

'Maybe you will,' Bathsheba said and their eyes met for the very first time and then looked away discomfited.

On their last day, at the end of rehearsals, the company stood formally in a queue to bid him goodbye, bearing little gifts, a mug with a picture of an apple, a key ring that had BROADWAY indented on brass and various picture postcards. Bathsheba stood very still, a rich amber amulet on her throat, held in a wide, black grosgrain band, gaiety and mourning as one. Her card was in an envelope and once out on the street, he opened it and leapt with excitement. It was a photograph of a bunch of rhubarb, tied in a posy, the thin vermilion stalks smothered in swathes of green. There was no message. On a tiny card was her address in Brooklyn and her apartment, 2a, but no telephone number.

An awakened passion in him suddenly extended to all mankind, including his wife and only the hardest heart could begrudge him such recklessness, as he hailed a taxi to take him uptown. At Central Park he leapt out, his heart opening to embrace traffic, fumes, frenzy, hurrying humanity and yes, even the soulless works of art nailed to the railings along Fifth Avenue. Insanely, he smelt orange blossom. It floated in from somewhere and in the garden of a restaurant, where he stopped to have a drink, the changing colour of Campari as the waiter added soda water seemed like a painting in the making. Back at the club for his farewells, he tipped lavishly and signed the visitors' book in a swirling hand.

Oonagh is bottling stemmed plums on the kitchen table and talking a mile a minute. The Clancy fella has been and blasted the rocks on the bit of field beyond their garden, so they would soon have a larger vegetable patch and her best hen, one of the Rhode Islands, had gone missing. Ownie, their neighbour's boy (a simpleton), had searched with her, high and low, calling and yodelling, but with no luck. Had he noticed the dahlias on the way in, and weren't they a sight to see, their blaze outdoing all the other flowers in the various beds. She had to know what the actors were like, how rehearsals went and if the director had approved of the adaptation they had done. She said they because she too had a part in *Vanya*, consulting with him on the different drafts. At times they acted it out together in the winter evenings, donning hats or scarves or stoles to emulate this or that character. One evening, as a celebration, Ownie and his mother were invited over for a surprise performance and Ownie had sat rigid throughout. Afterwards, the mother asked if the drunk Dr Astrov in the play was modelled on their local doctor, while Ownie wept helplessly, asking why everyone in the story was so unhappy in love.

'Did the two main actresses get on?' Oonagh is asking and suddenly Malachi is afraid, afraid of her wife's antennae.

'Of course they got on, they're professionals,' he said, that bit too snappy.

'You're a bag of cats, Malachi,' she said turning away, refusing to open the package in which there was a lace blouse that Bathsheba had helped him choose in an antique shop in Greenwich Village.

'I'm sorry . . . I'll sleep it off,' he said appeasingly, but then, just at the stairwell, she called after him to say they have been invited that evening to supper at Ewart's house. 'Creep.' Ewart, the reigning literary swell, whose star rose by the hour, while his fell. Ewart jetting in from some festival in Rome or Paris or Barcelona and, as always, throwing a bash. He could just picture it, the oak door held open with a boulder for the rustic effect, champagne in pewter cups on the hall table, big arrangements of shop flowers, scented candles, along with framed testimonials that Ewart had accrued from all over. He hated him for that and for the way he ingratiated himself with the local ladies, his smarm, the soft voice, the gifts, crystals specially chosen to complement each woman's astrological sign. That and the donations he gave for local lads who volunteered to be stretcher-bearers for the halt and the lame in Lourdes.

'You won't find me there,' he said and continued on up.

Not long after Oonagh had left, he came down, poured himself a large whiskey and went through the kitchen, into the garden. The night so still, deep stillness and 'a foliage of stars'. Wasn't that what Joyce called the wily Giacomo in his hour of temptation. Malachi would send Bathsheba his first novel that had the best of himself and of the haunted landscape that had shaped him. He thinks of her hands turning the pages, her feelings melting into his and before long, he is carried away, up there all alone, in the old schoolhouse that Oonagh and her brother helped him renovate. A muse had entered his life, the very elixir that he needed to write again. Oonagh had done so twenty-five years previous, with her hushed voice and skin so white that the veins on her chest were as fine as filigree. It was at a Bloomsday celebration in Dublin, after he had been given an award and guests were imploring Oonagh to sing. Suddenly she stood up, the scarlet colour running zigzag on the column of her neck, the voice tentative, then not, soaring, so much so that the cut glasses on the dining table trembled to her breath. You could hear a pin drop. When she came to the line that Joyce himself would have known – *Oh Gregory let me in* – every man at that table wanted her. It was how they met.

'I love you both,' he called out to the sweet-smelling meadow and the folded flowers, and having said it more than once, his conscience was at ease. He felt exhilarated, renewed, and with a confounding logic said that all was well now in the best of all possible worlds. He fetched another drink. His mind is made up. He will return to Providence, Rhode Island, for the three weeks of rehearsal, come home and be a good husband again. He hears Bathsheba's voice calling his name across seas, that and the music of her silvery bracelets, tinkling the air.

Things were normal but wintry. He was full of consideration, whistling merrily, his whistles saying, *Observe how contrite I am*, carrying in enough logs for a month, insisting on making a bouillabaisse from a very complicated recipe. It was the evening he decided to light a fire in his study that things erupted, as he knew they must. The chimney still smoked. Had he not told her the evening before he left for the States to get the chancer back from Mullingar and say all was not super-duper, that the hundred euros he had forked out was a waste and to please return and sweep it properly. Then she tells him that her sister Siobhan, always a bone of contention, was accompanying them to the Leonard Cohen concert at the end of the month. No way. Siobhan's very presence would mar it, her non-stop gabble, her dirndl skirt, her boots and cowboy hat, her vulgarity.

'I can't stand her,' he said.

''Tis mutual,' Oonagh replied and asked if he ever stopped to consider the effect he had on others, so caught up was he in his own superiority.

'It's this coffee-shop psychobabble,' he said, stung by her effrontery.

'People feel ill at ease with you Malachi . . . you are so above them all.'

'They talk bullshit.'

'They can't help it . . . they don't know any better and you're no

Chekhov . . . if you were you would see into their poor hurt souls and their poor hurt selves . . .'

'Why haven't you said this before?'

'To be the good little wife,' she said, then laughed shrilly, adding that when he came into the pub people shied away to avoid him.

'Brendan doesn't think this,' he said.

'He's too nice to tell you.'

'But you're telling me.'

'Yes I am . . . You're not the author you set out to be . . . You're embittered . . . You'd sell your soul to appear in print.'

He asked her to retract it, which she wouldn't, and then he struck her a hard, hating blow across the cheek and he struck her a second time and could hear her laughing, goading him as he lunged, striking her anywhere, everywhere, and then a crash as she tripped over a chair, gripping the edges of the table to find her way around it and escape him. At that very moment the door was pushed in and he heard the ridiculous startled clucking of a hen. As he steadied the overturned lamp, he saw that the shoulder of her pink camisole had got torn and half of a gold chain snagged on her brazier.

'Darling . . . you found her,' she said to Ownie, as fondly as if nothing untoward had been happening.

'She was under a big black pot in the field between the knackers and us,' he said and together they let the hen down on the floor, where idiotically it began to peck at the small grains of rose crystal that had got ground in the frenzy. The first car was pulling up outside in the yard and there were friendly beep-beeps, as the group arrived for her monthly book club. It was followed by a second car, then a third, voices calling across the yard in the dusk, guests carrying plates and dishes and bottles.

'Tell them to fuck off out of here,' he said.

'Malachi,' she said quietly, shielding the child from his obscenities and it was at that instant he freaked. He pulled Ownie from her, lugged him out the back door and told him to look up at the sky and the Milky Way and for all of his life to remember that the Milky Way was the scar left by Phaethon's mad passage in his father's chariot.

There were no stars. There was no Milky Way.

In his study, their laughs, their voices, galled. He walked to the window, then to the sofa bed, then changed into his wellingtons for the impending journey. In the rucksack that he kept there, he searched to make sure his toothbrush and shaving kit were in it. It was always packed for when he went to Dublin every two weeks, to take a writing workshop at the university. He had to go somewhere, but where. His brother lived further north with a shrew of a wife, both of them teetotal and dinner at six o'clock, but Christ, his brother was his brother and he'd go there.

All mankind might have died as he trudged home under a hazed moon, the field a swamp, his boots aswirl with water and wet to the skin. In the distance a donkey brayed pitiously.

The house was in darkness, the key under the bit of slate, as he knew it would be, and he let himself in quietly, or as quiet as a tall, inebriated man could. Oonagh would be asleep, so he plumped for the downstairs room, the domain of Siobhan, where her toiletries clogged the window ledge. He was awake long before breakfast, clutching the letter he had written to Oonagh: *I know that I am a cunt at times and that you are the only person I can tell.*

'I better get some grub going,' he said as she appeared in the kitchen.

'Suit yourself . . . I'm not hungry,' she said and as she bent down to get the dog's bowl, he touched her neck gently, contritely, and she flung his hand off as if it was a branding iron. He was unslept, remorseful and fed up. Taking a scone from the batch that had been brought the previous evening, he retreated to his study, intending to stay there and let things simmer down.

As if by clairvoyance, he went to his desk and pulled the drawer open, already trembling. It was where he kept things, mementos, conkers from some desultory boyhood walk, the acceptance letter for his first short story, his grandfather's clay pipe and the black

Mass card for their child, who would have been called Isabella, had she lived. He would never forget that time in the hospital, Oonagh begging to be left alone with her little mite, whom she placed naked across her naked heart, insisting that once they touched, she could instil life back into it. She was unhinged with grief and the drugs they had given her, but ever afterwards she swore that it did happen, that for an instant, the small fingers wrapped themselves around her thumb and clung, clung. He had gone out to have a smoke when the nurse came for him and how well and how ineradicably he recalled the hush of that night, pigeons in a line along the turret, cooing softly, the warm smell of their droppings and the hopelessness in the nurse's expression. For a long time, Oonagh withdrew into herself, barely speaking and once when he asked her, begged her, to open up to him, she said it would be wrong, it would be a profanity.

So there it was, in the serviette that he had taken from a restaurant in Greenwich Village, the draft of the letter that he was writing to Bathsheba, although her name did not appear on the page. Oonagh had been in there, he knew without knowing. She had read some of the idiocies he had put down: *O shining city, city full of dreams* (from Baudelaire) and his own dream in which he was nibbling her hair. He asked what were her favourite flowers and wondered if he might send her wood violets, with the clay hanging off the stem.

'I never touched her,' he said as he stormed back into the kitchen.

'Poor Malachi,' she said, her face ash-white.

'Nothing happened,' he said.

'Everything happened,' she replied.

'I'm not going back to America . . . I'm not going back . . . I swear.'

'It doesn't make a whit of difference . . . we've lived a lie for too long.'

'Trust me,' he said, pleading with her.

'A time will come when I'll thank her for getting her claws into you,' she said.

'She is a beautiful and wounded woman,' he said bluntly.

'Oh really? She must give you the limelight, or maybe she'll give you the child I failed to.'

'Maybe she will,' he said savagely and he saw her lower lip quiver uncontrollably and then she shut up, as if throttled. But she had not finished, she had not said all the cruel things that were in her heart.

If she had not left at that moment, what would have happened? But she did leave and he was glad of it. He walked through the downstairs rooms, talking, shaking, shouting, he kicked things, waste-paper baskets, her shoes, her cardigan and a velvet panel that had slipped down from one of the tall window shutters. What he did then he knew to be desperate. He pulled out the drawer, had to wrench it to free it completely, and emptied the contents onto the floor, including the letter he had meant to give her, to make a fire. Yet he did not go into the kitchen to fetch matches. Instead, he sat down, staring at these things and wept, wept for his own increasing isolation, for his wife's broken trust and for the woman he would never see again.

From the bonfire in the garden, hours later, furls of ash rose and scattered and the smell in the air was redolent of autumn.

A warm Saturday six weeks later and Malachi sat in the kitchen with a chair to the open door, Nestor in Sigmund Freud mode, ears cocked, letting out mewls of anticipation, already guessing that Oonagh was coming. In a dark suit with a white collar, he felt like a schoolteacher about to give his estranged wife a geography lesson. The map in its goldish frame was already on the table, to demonstrate to her. It was an old map, buff-coloured and rare, which he had bought years before in a second-hand bookshop. All the towns and townlands and rivers and bridges and churches of Ireland were marked in it, alongside scenes of battle and the places of massacre and the places of pilgrimage, each with its own perfectly executed image.

The crunch of her high heels on the gravel made him jump, even though he was the one who had asked her to come. She had moved further north and the address she gave him, while she sorted things out, was above a paint shop in a small town in Longford. One night, very late, he drove there just to see it, but all was in darkness and he drove home again.

She looked drawn and sat stiffly as a visitor might, Nestor licking her ankles through her stockings and her hands folded sedately.

'I have decided,' he began, hoping there was nothing in his voice of the preacher – 'I want us to tour Ireland with *Uncle Vanya* . . . I want it done here . . . not there.'

'You can't afford it,' she said.

'I can. I've talked to Brendan . . . he's going to approach people . . . the local council, the arch-council . . . he's certain he can get the funding . . . we'll bring Chekhov to all the little towns where people are crying out for it.'

'They're not crying out for it,' she said wearily, 'they play bingo.'

'I want to give something back,' he said, then blurted the names of small towns to which they would travel – Ardstraw, Ardbeg, Ballybough, Ballymoney, Ballysadare, Benlettery, Bengowan, Killybegs, Magilacuddy, Sneem, Schull – then suddenly put the map back on the table and also sat.

'In Yalta,' he began, the voice high-pitched and near hysterical, 'Chekhov wrote to his future wife Olga in Moscow and said, *It is nine o'clock of an evening and I am as lonely as a coffin.*'

'And what did she write back?' she asked wearily.

'We don't know,' he answered, then pleadingly, 'Will you do it, will you bring Chekhov to those poor wretches who have never heard of him?'

She did not reply.

They sat in silence, the sun coming and going in glancing shafts and not a word was said, and no knowing what was lost or what might yet be salvaged.

'Oh poor Malachi . . . you're mad . . . stone mad,' she said and he saw that her eyes were filling up with tears, but that she could not speak. He knew now that it was yes, she would come with him and a strange, overwhelming tenderness befell him.

They would cast their bread upon the waters and in one of those sleepy, forgotten towns, someone young or old would be quickened into life at encountering Chekhov for the very first time. ∎

Xan Rice, age twelve, outside Buxton House, Potchefstroom High School for Boys, 1987
Courtesy of the author

OLD SCHOOL

Xan Rice

L ate on a Sunday afternoon in August on the Highveld. The sky is
bright and cloudless and the air thin and cold. The road is clear.
I know this road.

The tabletop mine dumps, Johannesburg shrinking in the rear-
view mirror, Soweto to the right, Lenasia to the left. *Townships,
locations.* Do they even use those words any more?

At the crossroads the squatter camp is still there after all these years,
beneath a billboard where a politician promises FLUSHING TOILETS
FOR ALL. The urban sprawl yields to smallholdings and scrubland and
the landscape reveals its winter coat. Red-brown soil, sallow grass,
coils of smoke, a lick of flame. Black and white plastic bags stabbed
by barbed wire. A cordon of yellow police tape near a stop sign.

Ahead, a flash of silver. The finders-keepers guy! Hubcaps shed
by cars hurtling along the highway, dusted and buffed, displayed in
neat rows or mounted on sticks like giant metallic sunflowers.

The sinking sun turns to silhouettes the stripes of blue gums and
the towers of the gold mines, the deepest in the world, a sign says. It
is dark when I finally reach the town of Potchefstroom.

I first travelled this road in January 1987, a twelve-year-old boy
heading to a state-run boarding school. My mother in the passenger
seat, my father at the wheel, his elbow out the window, a cigarette

between his fingers. Me, nervous but mostly excited. My brother, two years older, quiet, knowing what was to come.

Nearly five years later I left the school and the road behind. It was the end of 1991, the last year of racially segregated education in South Africa, the dying days of apartheid. I only really knew one person who was not white.

In 1838, three years after leaving the Cape Colony, a wealthy sheep farmer named Andries Hendrik Potgieter and his Voortrekker followers halted their ox wagons on the banks of the Mooi River.

Quickly their laager became a settlement, a town, capital of the Boer's Zuid-Afrikaansche Republiek and then a battlefield prize. Volleys of gunfire in Potchefstroom in 1880 signalled the start of the First Anglo-Boer War, in which the Boers emerged triumphant. Two decades later the British returned to scorch the earth, burning homesteads and cornfields and slaughtering cattle. Colonial soldiers herded Boer women and children into a concentration camp in Potchefstroom, a tactic replicated across the Boer territories. More than 27,000 Afrikaners died in the camps, along with up to 20,000 black Africans who were separately confined.

At the end of the war, Lord Alfred Milner, the governor of the Transvaal and Orange River Colonies, sought to anglicise the defeated republics. He ordered the establishment of half a dozen English-language schools in Johannesburg, Pretoria and Potchefstroom. They were to be modelled on British institutions such as Eton and Harrow and staffed with young Oxbridge graduates.

The site chosen for the boys' school in Potchefstroom was the former concentration camp. The two areas where the flimsy tents had been pitched were marked out as a cricket oval and a rugby field. In between rose the handsome school building with its Cape Dutch facade.

'College', as Potchefstroom High School for Boys became known, opened in 1905 with the aim of producing young men 'who are responsible, self-disciplined, independent in their thinking, tolerant and well-mannered'.

The first house was named Granton, after the Edinburgh district where the headmaster grew up, and the second was called Milton. Buxton was the last to be built, a double-storey block in the far corner of the grounds, nearest the railway line. Pupils were allocated randomly between the three houses when they were accepted at the school. I was sent to Buxton, which had a reputation for being the most rebellious house, run more by the senior boys than the housemasters.

All the Buxton 'newboys' were directed to a large ground-floor dormitory called Dorm One where twenty metal-frame beds were arranged a foot apart in two facing rows. My parents carried in my trunk and packed my clothes into a tall metal locker. Outside on the grass I posed stiffly for a photograph in my uniform: brown shoes, grey trousers, white shirt, navy blazer with an orange springbok-horn badge and vertical yellow stripes, matching tie. On my head a straw boater several sizes too big.

The Buxton newboys were a motley bunch. Some, like me, came from the Witwatersrand. Others lived in the Orange Free State or blink-and-you-miss-it towns in Western Transvaal. There was a strapping boy from Botswana whose family owned a cattle farm and another one from Potchefstroom whose father bred chickens in such numbers that he owned a fleet of sports cars.

That first night we were each assigned as a fag to a matric, as the final-year pupils were known. For the next eleven months it would be our job to make his bed, polish his shoes, lay out his clothes in the morning, squeeze toothpaste onto his toothbrush, fetch him tea, procure snacks and sometimes cigarettes, and carry his books to and from class.

In the morning, lugging two satchels, the newboys hurried to the school buildings, five minutes away. The classrooms were arranged in a rectangle around the hall, into which we filed for assembly, the senior boys sitting on chairs, the rest of us on the floor. If we looked up at the walls we could read the names of 'Our Glorious Dead', old boys who died fighting for the Allies in the world wars or while

serving in the national army after South Africa became a republic in
1961. Higher still was an orange, white and blue South African flag
that had once flown over parliament, a gift to the school from the
local MP, a former minister of police.

After a Bible reading and a prayer we stood to sing a hymn from
the tiny blue songbooks that we all carried in our blazer pockets and
which served a dual purpose. At break the newboys swarmed around
the noticeboard and scrawled in the book margins the line-ups of
the first cricket, hockey and rugby teams. These we were obliged
to memorise, along with the house and school war cries, the school
song, and the names of all eighty or so matrics, who took it upon
themselves to test us.

This normally occurred after lunch when we returned to our
houses for roll call. The whole of Buxton assembled in Dorm One,
squeezing between the newboys' beds, which were often 'stripped',
the mattress exposed and the sheet and blanket and counterpane
tangled on top, because they had not been made neatly enough. The
duty prefect read out the names of those of us who had committed
other crimes: failing sweeping, bathroom or picking-up-rubbish duty;
not making it out of the house before the exit bell. A few matrics
then sifted through the letters pile, smelling any envelope from Potch
Girls' High to see if it was scented with perfume, before flinging it in
the direction of the intended recipient.

I wrote home every couple of days.

*Dear Mom and Dad. I have quite a few friends and get along
with everyone . . . I am sorry I could not speak to Dad or
you on the phone as I would have cried. Love from Xan
PLEASE WRITE SOON.*

*Dear Mom and Dad. The night before last I plugged locker
and bathroom locker inspection. I await my fate . . .*

Fate could mean many things. The worst was PT, a group punishment that involved push-ups, burpees and six-inch leg raises. Caning – with a cricket wicket, a length of bamboo, a plank – hurt more but was at least over quickly.

> *Dear Mom and Dad. We have been gated because someone went into his locker before the rising bell, so I cannot go downtown today or next weekend . . . I can't wait till the running is finished. It is hell.*

Athletics training at 5.30 a.m. was mandatory for the first month, until the inter-house competition. Then it was swimming, which was even tougher. Afternoons were reserved for team sports. Rugby was compulsory for first- and second-year pupils and not much fun unless you were big for your age or fast. Our opponents from the local Afrikaans schools played with an intensity that suggested revenge for the concentration camps.

In the evenings we walked back to school to do our homework and then checked in on our matric one last time. After lights out the house was finally silent and you could hear the chug of the night trains. One or two boys who still had the energy and guts or were simply incorrigible would risk showing off their bodily talents. Lying on their stomachs with their knees tucked and their naked bottoms high, they would suck in air through their anus and fart loudly. It was a trick only for the confident: in previous years a boy seeking glory expelled a solid instead of a gas. From then on his nickname was Shotgun.

On Sunday mornings we dressed in our school uniforms and boaters and walked to church. There were Anglican and Catholic churches in town but most of us claimed to be Methodists because the service lasted only forty-five minutes. We then had a few hours to kill downtown, though there was not much to do or see.

Even by South African standards, Potchefstroom was a deeply conservative place. The university prohibited social dancing on campus while Eugène Terre'Blanche's Afrikaner Weerstandsbeweging, the Afrikaner resistance movement, or AWB, a paramilitary group that regarded the apartheid government as too liberal, held regular meetings in town, an additional incentive, were any needed, for 'non-whites' to keep to their own areas, which were defined by law.

Beyond the railway line behind Buxton, beyond the industrial area, was the black African location of Ikageng. Coloureds (as people of mixed race are still known in South Africa) had their own township, Promosa, and South Africans of Indian descent lived in Mohadin.

To us these were just names. We never went there, never played sport against their schools and seldom saw their inhabitants. We knew nothing about these people of other races.

The prejudice towards them was blind and entrenched in language. Indians were *currymunchers*, *charras*, *canecutters*, *coolies*. Coloureds were *point-fives*. Black people were *pekkies*, *coons*, *munts*, *zots*, *spoons*, *spades*, *kaffirs*. A boy who chewed with his mouth open or who failed to put on deodorant was reminded of his superior colour: 'White skin!' If a junior was cocky rather than subservient to someone in a higher grade he was accused of 'being white'. Anyone who suggested black people were treated unjustly was a *kaffirboetie*, a *kaffir* brother.

Racial slurs were used by pupils of all ages, among themselves. Teachers did not encourage such language, and seldom, if ever, spoke this way in front of us. But they also made little attempt to stamp it out. It was coarse, macho talk, but it was not simply boys being boys. Many of the children would have first heard these words at home.

Kids with dark skin were often mocked about having mixed blood. One Granton boy in my year was given the nickname Naidoo – a common surname in Indian townships – and a Milton boy was sometimes called Kaffir K. If you had tight curly hair you would be reminded of the 'pencil test'. The apartheid authorities had used this method to determine racial identity: if a pencil pushed into a person's hair did not fall out, he or she was classified as coloured.

In the dining hall we sat at tables of eight, seven boys from the same year and a matric. He would eat as much as he wanted, with the remaining food passed around anticlockwise. Some table heads would enforce a rule where the boy to his right served himself as much as he liked, which meant the last boy received little or no food. This was called the *kaffir* system, because that's how black people supposedly behaved, with greed and no self-control. In a similar way, a boy who spread too much peanut butter on his bread would be accused of 'going *kaffir*'. Housemasters and teachers frowned on this kind of behaviour but rarely found out about it. 'Spying' – telling someone in authority about wrongdoing – was taboo among the boys.

Several dozen black men and women worked at the school, travelling by bicycle from Ikageng to clean the houses, prepare the sports fields, cook our food. Most were invisible to us or at least to me – to this day I have no recollection of any black women at the school.

The few black staff we regularly came into contact with worked in the dining hall. We called teachers sir or ma'am and older boys by their surnames but the black staff we addressed by their first names. Daniel and Sam, who liked to talk about football; Abe, the quiet, older man with a deep dent in his forehead; Danny *Bosluis* – Danny the tick – who had a bad limp and a perpetual frown.

Since much of the food was unpalatable – liver, overcooked greens, Welsh rarebit – we gorged on bread at mealtimes. When the bread tin was empty one of us would hold it up for a refill. If it were Danny Bosluis who approached, the matric would sometimes order the boy to drop the tin just as Danny reached out for it. Clang! The dining hall fell silent and everyone stared at Danny.

The most popular black worker, especially with the younger boys, was Solly, who had a wicked sense of humour and a foul mouth. He rightly called us 'fucking philistines'.

This was what I knew about Solly.

He was short and had a very long fingernail on one hand. He owned an old Ford Cortina that he had painted yellow. He never missed a first-team rugby match. He was at ease among whites at the school, including teachers and parents. He had been given a watch for long service.

These were some of the things I did not know.

Solly was one of twelve siblings. He had four children. He had a primary-school education and spoke six languages. Beyond the school gates he was scared of white people, knowing he could be beaten for no reason and could not retaliate. He especially feared the police, who could be cruel in so many ways. Once, after throwing him in the back of a pickup for breaking the town's 8 p.m. curfew for non-whites, the officers stopped at a corner shop en route to the police station. They put six large jam doughnuts and a big mug of coffee in front of Solly and said he was free to leave if he could finish it all quickly. He tried and he failed and they laughed and laughed and then got bored and said to him: 'Go!'

A t the end of my first year several Buxton newboys left the school because they were homesick or unwilling to put up with the bullying. It was the same the following year. By the third year though, school was tolerable, even enjoyable, especially if you liked sport and were content to conform.

When the shower drain blocked and the water overflowed into the communal urinal we no longer had to stamp in the soapy piss to ease the blockage – there were newboys for that. Our fear of matrics was manageable and the main threat of punishment came from the male teachers. The principal took this responsibility especially seriously. In his office he kept a hardcover exercise book that had been passed down by the various heads since 1956 and recorded the name of every boy caned, the number of lashes and the offence.

> P.R. 4. Disgraceful behaviour – suggestive language and
>   vulgarity to a girl of a visiting school.
> J.P. 4. Pornographic literature at school. Final warning.
> R.B. 4. Drinking liquor.
> I.R. 2. Cadets – undisciplined.

Cadets was a mandatory and much-loathed programme at most white secondary schools, overseen by the South African Defence Force. Every Monday we would change into khaki uniforms and march in military formation around the rugby field for an hour. The aim was to boost national pride and forge early loyalty to the armed forces. All white males over seventeen had to report for two years of military service. Some boys had brothers in the army, so we knew what that would entail: patrolling the townships or fighting the covert war in Angola.

There was further indoctrination during veld school, a week-long camp that fifteen-year-old white schoolchildren across the Transvaal attended. An experience that could have been fun – learning bush craft, cooking over fires – was dulled by the propaganda: singing the national anthem every morning while the flag was raised, the lectures about the threat of Satan, communism and, most dangerous of all, the black terrorists.

The only black person I knew well was Isabel Manana. My mother had met Isabel while teaching black men and women to read and write at a church in Johannesburg, and asked if she wanted a job as a housekeeper. The Group Areas Act forbade blacks from living in white-designated urban areas but an exception was made for domestic workers, or 'maids' as they were called. And so, when I was seven, Isabel moved into a small self-contained room behind our garage. While my mother was out managing a big supermarket, Isabel washed, vacuumed and ironed. She also made endless pots of tea for my father, a professional carpenter who built everything from kitchens to staircases and electric guitars, and emerged from his workshop several times a day smelling of sawdust and tobacco. But much of Isabel's time was spent looking after me and my two brothers, cleaning up our mess, settling our disputes, cooking us porridge for breakfast and meatballs with tomato and onion sauce and rice for dinner. We loved her, and gave her hell.

Visiting Isabel in her room one day we noticed that her bed was raised on bricks. She explained it was for protection against the *tokoloshe*, a dwarf-like creature that attacked its victims at night. We found this hilarious. 'Isabel, the *tokoloshe* is coming for you,' we'd say over and over again. She would threaten to beat us, and then join in the laughter. Her bed remained on bricks.

Isabel had six children of her own and every few months one of them would appear at the gate. Freddy and Patricia, the two eldest, were at a distant boarding school. Sharon, Cynthia, Zanele and S'fiso, then just a few years old, lived in KwaNdebele, one of the Bantustans established by the apartheid regime to keep black people far away from the whites. The four of them stayed in a single-bedroom house that Isabel had built. At the end of every month she travelled by taxi and then bus for seven hours to bring them food and money. The separation caused Isabel great pain but there was little choice. The exemption for domestic workers to live in white areas did not apply to their children.

Soon after moving in with us Isabel fell pregnant again. Her husband had never offered her much support previously and now he disappeared. By the time Isabel learned he had taken up with another woman she had given birth to a daughter she named Zandile.

After a long discussion with Isabel my parents decided that the law should be ignored. 'Zed', as we took to calling the baby, would stay with Isabel and be raised on our property.

Few College boys followed the goings-on in government, where the National Party had ruled for forty years. One of the only politicians we all knew of was the cantankerous, finger-wagging president, P.W. Botha, known as *die groot krokodil*, the big crocodile, because of his stubbornness and ability to outmanoeuvre opponents.

Then, in 1989, Botha suffered a stroke. In February 1990, the new president, F.W. de Klerk, ordered that Nelson Mandela be released after twenty-seven years in jail, and unbanned the African National Congress. I don't remember it being a big deal at school, but then there was no reason for it to have been. In history, my favourite subject, we had studied the rise of the Transvaal and the Orange Free State, the Anglo-Boer Wars and twentieth-century national politics – white politics. Black political history was almost entirely absent from the syllabus. This was before the Internet, and in the houses we did not watch television news. Even if we had it would not have made much difference, for broadcasters were restricted to showing what the government approved. The school library only stocked books passed by the censors, and every year a few titles, such as *Mao Tse Tung and the Chinese Communist Revolution*, were stamped CANCELLED and added to the pile of banned literature in the storeroom.

Democratic elections were still four years away and there was no immediate impact on our lives at school or beyond. But it was clear that something had changed. The government's admission that apartheid was wrong had made it acceptable, even fashionable, for white people to echo this publicly.

Towards the end of each year the school prize-giving was held in a lecture hall at the university. The headmaster would make a speech and so would an old boy. In 1989, a few months before Mandela's release, the speakers talked of the dangers of the occult and corruption, but did not mention racial injustice. A year later the old boy told us that we had to accept that there was a 'vast majority of South Africans who have keenly felt grievances and who have benefited very little from the economic growth that took this country to where it is today'. And the headmaster spoke of how the 'cry for freedom' had been heard all over the world.

By then, I was about to start matric. That final year, 1991, I was head boy of Buxton and had my own study and two newboys as my fags. Instead of spending Saturday mornings being forced to watch the first cricket team, I was among the players being applauded from the boundary. A letter from the army arrived saying that I had been called up for duty but I binned it since I planned to go university and students were granted deferrals.

That September, all the parents were asked to vote on the school's future admission policy and 85 per cent of them chose a model where boys of all races would be allowed to attend. The following January the first non-white boys walked through the gates of College.

Hundreds of other white schools across the country opened their doors to blacks, coloureds and Indians in 1992. For Isabel's six eldest children the change came too late. Black schools had been so starved of resources that most pupils were far behind white boys and girls of the same age.

But Zandile had a chance. She was only eight and had the option of going to Blairgowrie Primary School at the end of our road, which my brothers and I had attended. After an assessment she was accepted, though she had to drop a grade. She quickly caught up academically and excelled at athletics and swimming. In the afternoons she and a classmate whose mother was also a domestic worker would play in our pool.

By the time Zandile started secondary school both my brothers had left home, though I was still there. One day my mother asked Zandile if she wanted to move out of Isabel's room and into a vacant bedroom next to mine, where she would have space to study and could decorate as she pleased. Zandile did not need to be asked twice. It was strange for a week or two, for me and for Zandile, who kept largely to herself. But it soon became normal.

My last trip to College was in August 1993, the day my father died of a heart attack. My mother and I drove through the night to Potchefstroom to fetch my younger brother. I remember the silence and the darkest sky and seeing a shooting star that we agreed was Dad.

Eight months later I voted in the first democratic elections to be held in South Africa. Mandela became president. The struggle against apartheid was over, a struggle that I had never been part of. Had I been born ten or twenty years earlier I would have taken risks, fought the injustice. That's what I told myself back then.

The struggle was not over, though. At the University of the

Witwatersrand, where I was studying, there were occasional disturbances to lectures and protests over the financial and academic exclusion of black school leavers, an issue that has blown up again today. The easy option was to ignore their plight, and I did.

After graduating I joined the accounting firm KPMG, which, like other companies, had suddenly taken in a lot of black trainees in a bid to appear less white. I was friendly with most of the young black men and women in my business unit, but the friendship was never deep. I started to learn Zulu and then took up French instead – there was a world beyond South Africa. At the end of 1999 I quit my job and boarded a plane for London. My plan was to make some quick money, go backpacking and figure out what I wanted to do with my life. I was sure I would be back.

Seventeen years have passed since I left South Africa. I visit each year for a few weeks to see my mother, my brothers, my in-laws. Each time the country feels a little more foreign and the prospect of a permanent return more remote. I have a family now, and my children are English.

After my departure I saw Isabel and Zandile a few times, but only fleetingly. When I called Isabel last summer she said she now lived at her rural home, where her kids grew up, and we arranged to meet there. On a Sunday morning I drove north from Pretoria, into the countryside where cows and ostriches shared fields and two rivers, Elands and Crocodile, ran dry. Soon I was in the former Bantustan of KwaNdebele, which remains a black area. By the roadside churchgoers walked with purpose, women in their blue and white blouses and dresses, men in white trousers and purple blazers. Small shops advertised haircuts, car parts, chicken milk soap and burial services.

Zandile met me in the town of Moteti. We hugged and I told her she looked like a Boer in her silver-grey Chevrolet pickup.

'You have to be practical, hey!' she replied.

I followed her to Isabel's home, along a dirt road. When Isabel ran out of the house laughing with joy, her arms wide open, I burst into tears. It took several minutes to compose myself. '*Hawu*, Xanny, it's okay my boy,' Isabel said, arm around me, as we sat in her living room.

Several of Isabel's children and other relatives had joined us in the living room. They looked on in silence, and with concern, unsure what had happened.

What had brought on the emotion? Was it love? Was it guilt, or shame, at not having kept in closer contact with someone who had been such a big part of my upbringing? This was the first time I had ever visited her home.

Isabel proudly showed me around her house, which now had four bedrooms instead of one. In the kitchen stood a half-barrel of *umqombothi*, a creamy traditional beer, left over from the wedding of Isabel's fifth-born child Zanele the day before. All around were relics of our old house: two fridges, my late grandmother's floral tapestry, a wooden seahorse carved by my father, the metal trunk from my College days.

We chatted for a while about the past, the funny and the sad times – the death of her son Freddy and her daughter Patricia, who was murdered in Soweto in the nineties. My mother made several trips to the township with Isabel to try to find Patricia's remains. The hospital that had treated her refused to say where the body was, to avoid being implicated in her death. There had been a nurses' strike at the time of Patricia's admission and she might otherwise have survived her injuries.

'Don't write that down, Xanny,' Isabel said. 'I don't want to get into trouble.'

Zandile interjected: 'Mom, it's a long time ago. You can't get into trouble now. Tell your stories.'

Isabel was entrepreneurial – she set up several microbusinesses while working for us – but ultimately the job of a housekeeper for a white family had been her ceiling. Even after finishing school, I never talked to her about apartheid, what she had been denied. I asked her now if she ever felt bitterness about those years of white oppression and the question seemed to catch her off guard. She frowned, seeming almost angry.

'No. Shame! Who will I get cross for? The past is gone and it won't come back again. I don't have any stress now, Xanny.'

Isabel wanted to make me tea even though there was a water outage in the area. While she tried to find some water, I sat down alone with Zandile, who is now thirty-three, and has a successful career working for an airline in Johannesburg. She had driven down for the wedding with her eight-year-old son. Her siblings S'fiso and Cynthia were also there, and it was clear that Zandile and Cynthia in particular were close. It had not always been so.

The decision to allow Zandile to stay with Isabel had caused resentment among the other children, who felt she was being unfairly favoured. Only recently had the rift repaired, Zandile said. 'They saw me as privileged, which I was compared to them. But I was the poor kid in a privileged environment.'

Zandile said that as a child she could not understand why she had to move to a 'white' school in 1992, away from all her friends, and where she was on occasion called a monkey. Secondary school was better, but she still felt like an outsider. I always assumed Zandile had enjoyed school. So too did my mother, who was deeply saddened when I told her what Zandile said. In the unspoken words between people of different races, back then and perhaps now too, so much was hidden.

In the early afternoon we all posed for a photograph outside Isabel's house, and then I said goodbye and set off on the long drive to College, past the tabletop mine dumps, Soweto to the right, Lenasia to the left.

The next morning I drove from my hotel on the outskirts of Potchefstroom to the school. The streets were familiar even if the names had changed: Govan Mbeki Avenue, Nelson Mandela Drive, Sol Plaatje Street. The main thoroughfare that led to College was called Dr James Moroka Avenue – a name I did not recognise. Later, when I read up on Moroka, I learned he was a medical doctor who served as president of the African National Congress between 1949 and 1952. He had earned his degree at the University of Edinburgh, and opened his practice on a farm in the Orange Free State, serving blacks as well as Afrikaners, including some who were spurred to overcome their racial prejudice because they had contracted venereal disease and were too embarrassed to visit their white doctor.

A bitter wind blew and when I arrived at the school a few boys in their striped blazers and ties huddled against a sunlit wall eating quarter-loaves of bread stuffed with chips. The receptionist told me it was break time and directed me to the staffroom, where the teachers were drinking coffee. I spotted John Swanepoel, the deputy headmaster, who twenty-six years earlier had taught me science. He did not have any classes for the rest of the day and agreed to show me around the school.

Behind the staffroom was a smart new lecture theatre. The large bell in the courtyard that was rung to signal the start of class had been replaced by an electronic one, and the metalwork room was now the computer centre, but for the most part the school buildings and fixtures looked just like they had when I left, if a bit more worn. There was the hall, with its high ceilings and the lists of Our Glorious Dead. There was the noticeboard, still displaying the line-ups of the first sporting teams for the boys to memorise.

There was one major change, though. There were hardly any white boys at the school, even though all but two of the thirty or so teachers were still white.

When we sat down in his office, Swanepoel gave me the numbers: out of 468 pupils, five were white. Another fifteen or so were Indian South Africans, or originally from elsewhere in Asia. The rest were coloured or black, including some from other southern African countries.

'Are we a black school now? I'd say so,' Swanepoel said. 'But it's still recognised as a good school, one of the best in North West province.'

This was true: the son of the province's premier is a matric and African National Congress secretary general Gwede Mantashe had recently sent two of his boys to College. There have been insinuations, mostly from white old boys, that standards have fallen, but the matric results from 2015, when 96 per cent of pupils passed and one in two were accepted into university, were virtually unchanged from 1995, when the school was still overwhelmingly white.

Swanepoel suggested we tour the houses, which are now separated by grade to try to prevent bullying by seniors.

In Milton House the matron's office was crowded with boys spreading peanut butter and jam on slices of brown bread for a mid-morning snack, just as we had done.

'Boys, break is cancelled,' Swanepoel said.

'*Hawu*, sir!' the pupils said, alarmed, before realising he was joking.

Buxton, my old house, was awaiting renovations, and had plenty of space, since most College pupils are now day boys. Even so, the bathrooms were unrecognisable: instead of communal showers there were individual stalls, and urinals had replaced the long metal piss trough. The era of stamping to ease blockages was long gone.

Swanepoel knocked on the door of my old study. Hearing no answer, we entered. A head appeared from beneath a duvet. Instead of swotting for exams, which the matrics were writing, the boy had been sleeping.

Swanepoel, an Afrikaner who had served in the army and ran the school's cadet programme in my day, looked disgusted but said nothing. The pupils no longer feared the teachers, and discipline at the school had slipped, he said.

From what I saw and heard at the school Swanepoel was well respected by the boys and his fellow teachers. But his stern manner – a trait even when I was at College – had sometimes led people to wonder about his views. Swanepoel told me that he was once asked by a black pupil whether he was a racist. When he said yes, the boy replied, 'So how can you be here?' And Swanepoel said: 'Because I don't discriminate against anyone based on colour.'

I must have looked confused because he tried to explain.

'I worry about the future of this country. But I am not this AWB guy who wants to plant bombs. On the street I call a black man sir. If a white boy disrespects me I feel exactly the same as when a black boy does. But if you ask me if I am a racist by heart, I have to say yes. I don't think there's a single country in the world where you have more than one race and find no racism.'

S wanepoel's admission shocked me. Not just what he said, but also his honesty, a brave honesty, I thought. Apartheid had marked him, as it has marked all of us, in different ways. It made me hyper-aware of colour. Even today, a person's skin tone is the first thing I consciously process when seeing him or her for the first time.

The next morning as I walked across the school quadrangle one of the teachers collared me. Bev Johnson arrived at College in 1993, after I left, but she knew my younger brother. She had heard I was researching a story and seemed concerned that I did not fully understand the history of colonialism and apartheid. 'We have so much to answer for,' Johnson said.

Her sense of guilt was as strongly expressed as the denial of it by Swanepoel, a fellow white teacher who had lived in the same town and through the same changes in South Africa and at College since the end of minority rule. Johnson needn't have worried about expressing her feelings since they chimed with my own. Ever since I left the country I have felt lingering pangs of conscience at having departed without ever helping to heal its wounds. But there was a difference. By teaching at what had become a black school, Johnson *was* trying to play her part, as was Swanepoel. Both could easily have got jobs at schools where most pupils were white, had they wished, or sought employment overseas, as I had done.

Johnson asked me to address her class of first-year pupils, and thrust an exercise book into my hand, suggesting I look at the excellent quality of the work while she prepared her pupils for my talk.

Johnson waved me in to her classroom, the same one where I had sat twenty-nine years before listening to the art teacher warning that unless we behaved he would hit us *so hard that your eyes will pop out like Smarties.*

'Boys, stand and say good morning to Mr Rice, who is going to speak to you about his work.'

'Good morning, sir.'

They listened politely as I explained that I attended College in the whites-only days, now lived in England and was writing a story about how the school had changed. Johnson asked the boys if they had any questions. A few hands shot up.

'Sir, how does the school compare to when you were here?'

'How was the food back then, sir?'

'Sir, were you allowed to visit the girls' school in your time?'

'Sir, what were the matrics like?'

'How many countries have you visited, sir?'

'Did you have the same uniform as us, sir?'

I answered as best I could, but one left me puzzled.

'Have you ever been to Derbyshire, sir?'

I looked at Johnson. She smiled and said: 'His surname is Derbyshire.'

A few of the questions reminded me of the materialism that is so prevalent in South Africa – what was the most expensive watch I'd seen in England, what cars do people drive there – and also of the comfortable backgrounds of some of the pupils.

Though College has an open-admission policy and charges lower fees than the top private schools, its facilities and exam results are far better than the typical government school, especially in the former townships, making it attractive to middle- and upper-class black parents.

More than two decades after Mandela was elected, the state-run education system is in crisis, and the idea of equal opportunities for all remains a distant dream. In my day, the defining factor in determining a child's prospects was race: College was an elite school because it was a white school. Today it is class. My old school remains exclusive because many people cannot afford it.

Even so, there are kids there from poor families whose parents or relatives are making big sacrifices to give them a good education.

When the bell rang and the pupils filed out, Johnson asked one of them to stay behind, a serious-looking boy named Tumelo.

'Tumelo, tell Mr Rice about your parents.'

'I don't have any parents, sir.'

He explained that he lived with his grandmother in Promosa, the old coloured township. It was his maths exercise book that I had looked at while I was waiting for the class to be ready.

What had happened to Solomon Mokoena – Solly – the kitchen worker who called us philistines? From the College website I learned that he had retired in 2015 after forty-six years' service. The headmaster gave me Solly's mobile number and when I called he told me that he lived in a village about two and a half hours' drive from the school. The nearest big town was Rustenburg, and we agreed to meet there one morning.

I got lost and was forty-five minutes late. 'For fuck's sakes, man!' Solly said by way of greeting. He looked spry and was dressed as if he was about to drive one of the sports teams to a match: Reebok cap, blue FIRST TEAM HOCKEY tracksuit top, beige trousers. He suggested we talk at the home of his youngest daughter Grace.

Summer Breeze Estate was one of several new smart housing developments on the edge of town. What sorts of people live there? 'White, black, pink, blue, green – anyone who can afford to,' Solly said.

Grace, who was born in Potchefstroom when I was at College, was married to a safety officer at a nearby platinum mine. She ribbed her father for getting her birth year wrong – 'It's his age, *neh!*' – and left us alone in the lounge to chat.

Solly explained that he was born in Vredefort, a town in the Orange Free State, where his parents worked for an Afrikaner farmer who kept cattle and grew corn. As the child of a black farmworker, Solly had no opportunity to attend secondary school.

In 1966, when he was sixteen, his father found work on a farm in Potchefstroom and moved his family there. Solly did odd jobs for two years before a friend told him of a house-cleaning position at College. He moved into a ten-bed dormitory in a house in Ikageng, the black township, and cycled through the dark streets to the school at 4 a.m. to shovel coal into the boilers for the showers.

After a few years the headmaster allowed Solly to move into a small room on the College grounds. He married one of the cleaners, Lena, and started a family. They weren't permitted to keep their children at school, which was an officially white area, and so sent them to live in Bophuthatswana, the Bantustan where Solly's parents had moved.

He recounted the story about the police and the doughnuts, and spoke of his fear of the white man during the apartheid days. But he said had never experienced racism at the school, from either the teachers or the pupils. Could that really have been the case, given the way the boys talked among themselves? And if it was not, why didn't he tell me? But what reason would he have to confide in me – someone he probably did not remember from College and who had only looked him up twenty-five years later?

'In my life, from being born until now, the best place was College,' Solly said. A place where he could not live with his kids because of the colour of their skin. 'I went from being a boy to an old man there.'

He had outlasted many of his colleagues. Danny Bosluis, dead. Abe, the sad-looking waiter, dead. Sam, the jovial footballer, dead, Solly told me. There was some continuity, though: his great-nephew Neo was a matric at the school, one of South Africa's 'born free' generation who, unlike their parents, had never known apartheid.

After two hours or so, the conversation dried up and I sensed Solly was a bit bored of telling his story. We ate lunch at a fast-food joint and then set off for Mmatau, his rural village in the former Bophuthatswana, ninety minutes' drive away. I asked if I could get him anything to say thank you for his time and he said 'medicine'. A few miles on he said, 'There's a pharmacy,' and we went inside. He chose a bottle of Richelieu brandy and eight bottles of Carling Black Label beer. Soon the first empty Carling flew out of Solly's window, smashing by the roadside. He opened up a bit more.

'In the old days I could never have just walked into that shop and bought brandy. We were not allowed inside a liquor store: I would have had to ask a white to go in for me.

'*Ag*, it was a bad time.'

As we neared Mmatau the terrain became ever more harsh, with rocky hills and thorn trees. The tarmac road gave way to dirt. Solly's small house stood in the middle of a large plot of red sand. Several of his relatives were enjoying the late-afternoon sun around the back.

While no one was looking, Solly took the remaining beers and the brandy bottle inside and hid them. The sun was about to set and the road conditions would be hazardous because of the potholes, animals crossing and the aggressive driving of other motorists. Solly asked me to phone him when I reached my hotel that night so he could be sure I'd arrived safely. I forgot and so he called me. I felt bad when I picked up, but he did not want an apology, just to know that I was okay. Still looking after his boys.

The politician Julius Malema – the one who promised FLUSHING TOILETS FOR ALL on the squatter camp billboard – said recently that he knew democracy was working when homeless whites begged him for money. By that measure, South Africa *is* more democratic than when I lived there. In Rustenburg, white men guarded vehicles in parking lots for tips. Outside a supermarket in Potchefstroom, a young Afrikaner asked me to buy him a pie because he was hungry.

Filling up my car with petrol near the school one afternoon, I was approached by a black man who asked if I would buy a sponge or a cloth from him for fifteen rand. I bought a cloth.

Then an older white man with a sun-scarred face came to my window and pushed a pen into my hand. Twenty rand, he said. While I was taking the money out of my wallet he dropped a second pen on my lap. Buy two, he said.

I was angry – rather than being grateful, he was aggressive. But it was more than that. I felt less sorry for the white man. He had enjoyed the benefits of apartheid and had blown it. Of course this was unfair – there were poor whites under apartheid, and who knew what had happened to this man to put him in the situation he was. But my instinct dictated otherwise.

A related impulse influences my behaviour in shops and restaurants whenever I visit South Africa. I am extra polite and friendly to black workers, making jokes, saying multiple thank-yous. Trying to connect in some way. Ordering lunch at a takeaway burger joint in Potchefstroom, I chatted to the black woman cashier while the other customers – a father and son built like oxen and wearing rugby shorts and khaki shirts, a middle-aged woman straight from the hair salon – stood silently waiting for their food. In the cashier's face I sensed a slight unease at my attempts at conversation: it was the sort of look a tourist in a foreign land receives when he talks too loudly or asks the wrong question.

Maybe that's what I am now: a foreigner with a local accent.

During mid-morning break one day three boys walked over for a chat. They were good sportsmen, a hockey player, a cricketer and a rugby player. We talked about the excellent facilities: the immaculate cricket and rugby fields with inbuilt sprinkler systems, the cricket bowling machines, the gym, the renovated squash courts. The hockey player wondered if the school would ever get an AstroTurf pitch, like some of the bigger schools. Then he changed the subject.

'Sir, do you think white boys will ever come back?'

I said I was not sure, and asked if it mattered.

'It does, sir. We need them. It will help with our language.'

Most of the black pupils speak Setswana at home and when chatting to their friends at school. But it was not an exam subject – English and Afrikaans remain the two compulsory languages in the South African education system.

Unlike the paucity of black teachers, which none of the pupils raised with me as an issue, the absence of white pupils greatly concerned the College boys. The previous day outside Bev Johnson's class another pupil had asked me a similar question about the possible return of white kids in big numbers.

Johnson had tried to explain to him why this was unlikely. First, only 10 per cent of South Africans are white, she said. Second, the school was now expensive for boarders (in my day, fees were very low), and most white pupils had historically stayed in the houses because they lived outside Potchefstroom.

Furthermore, white English-speaking people with the means were also increasingly choosing private schools for their children.

I was still thinking about what the boys had said about white pupils when I went to the town library to do research and make photocopies that afternoon.

A smartly dressed young black man was in charge of the computer and copy centre. It turned out he was also a College old boy. Oatile Sitase told me that he started at the school in 2004, when it was still racially diverse. His friendship circle included two black boys, two white boys and two Chinese. 'Even today we still talk and have braais. They are my eyes and I am their eyes in terms of jobs,' he said.

While reading I had noticed a black boy, a coloured boy and a white boy sitting at a table doing their homework together. Now, on leaving the library, I saw a chunky blond teenager and a thin black kid of a similar age walking down the street, laughing and chatting. Both boys wore the uniform of Volkies, a local Afrikaans school. As I watched them I felt a dull ache develop in my chest. I was physically heartsore: filled with envy, sadness, anger at opportunities denied, missed.

And I suddenly understood what the black boys had been saying about wanting white boys at College. It was not really about language or the perception of the school. It was about not being apart. ∎

Travel writing isn't dead; it can no more die than curiosity or humanity or the strangeness of the world can die. If anything, it's broken out of its self-created shell, as more and more women give us their half of the world, and Paris is ever more crowded with visitors from Chengdu. When I was growing up, travel reportage used to smack of a somewhat colonial transaction, in which visitors from the privileged countries inspected the 'natives' of less materially fortunate places, from Patagonia to Kashmir. These days it consists of young writers from India – Anjan Sundaram, Samanth Subramanian, Rahul Bhattacharya – illuminating from within the Congo, Sri Lanka or Guyana, while Americans from Paul Theroux to Bill Bryson observe the quaintness of the 'natives' of Great Britain.

Of course there are forty people crossing international borders these days for every one in 1960; go to the Golden Temple in Kyoto, and what you'll likely see are the (literally) 50 million tourists who visit Japan's ancient capital every year. All that means, however, is that exoticism takes new forms today. If you wish to catch Istanbul in the twenty-first century, you're better off in the Kanyon Mall than in the Grand Bazaar; perhaps the most eye-opening foreign country I ever visited was Los Angeles International Airport, where once I spent two weeks wandering the terminals, watching the global city of the future form and re-form around me.

I sit now in the high mountain sunshine of Bhutan, surrounded by dark chapels filled with butter lamps – encircled by signs for iPhone repair shops and Baskin-Robbins ice cream – and I'm reminded that our jobs as recorders of the world have changed a little: the writer on place, like every writer, has to think consciously today about what she can do with words that no YouTube video bringing Havana with screaming vitality into our bedrooms can do better, and how she can evoke the noiseless valleys around Punakha in ways no digital camera can match.

The writer on place has to go further inward, into the realm of silence and nuance and personal enquiry. But that has always been the heart of the enterprise: Ryszard Kapuściński wrote about Iran or Ethiopia as a stealthy, coded way of weighing the consequences of repression in his native Poland; V.S. Naipaul wandered the post-colonial world to make sense of the colonising culture – and the colonised soul – within. My only sorrow right now is that the kind of confident and masterful portraiture provided by Jan Morris is almost impossible to find in our more cautious, first-person, reality-show age. Anecdote is fast eclipsing analysis, and blogs that read like children's 'What I Did on My Summer Holidays' essays supplant the kind of piercing, rigorously researched, fearless descriptions that acknowledge that places are at least as alive as people are.

But that doesn't mean that travel writing is dead; only that we sometimes are. ■

It sometimes seems to me that all my writing is travel writing. Perhaps this is because I have moved so much in my life: most of my first decade was spent in California, my second in Lahore, my third in New York, my fourth in London, and my fifth, thus far, in Lahore again.

Or perhaps it is because I still travel so often. I am a very frequent flyer. When I arrive in a new place, I fantasise about settling there. When I return again to my house, my house appears strange to me, and I detect in myself ongoing impulses to move away.

I think I am a kind of nomad. A seafarer who feels unsettled when he disembarks on dry land. Certainly I am a migrant – even though I live where I was born, and my children are the fourth generation of our family to while away their afternoons on our house's shady lawn.

Increasingly, I have come to believe that we are all migrants, that the experience of migration unites all human beings, that movement through time is our shared journey, indeed that to be a human being is to be just that, a human being, being first in this moment, then in that, then in the one after, and so on, for a lifetime. Constantly in motion, constantly journeying, even when seemingly in repose.

Travel is universal. So what matters to me is not whether a piece of writing is called travel writing. What matters is the writing itself. What it does. What it says. Nothing more, and nothing less. ∎

The fun thing about questions like this is that you can substitute any word or term for 'travel writing' with no diminution of the urgency of the enquiry. Some years ago, for example, I spoke at a conference in San Francisco dedicated to the question 'Is photography over?' In the end we weren't sure. Yes and no. Sort of. And the same is true here.

Two forms of travel writing do seem sufficiently well-worn that they've become the literary equivalent of package tours in which destination and experience are so thoroughly predetermined that one is reluctant to make a booking. These would be: 1. *In the Footsteps of . . .* where a writer recreates journeys made by someone or other and observes the changes that have taken place in the terrain while also telling the story of the antecedent's life and work. 2. *On a . . .* where a writer chooses a deliberately impractical mode of transport, thereby inviting the calamities that will inevitably befall him or her. Something along the lines of *Round South America on a Pogo Stick*. Naturally, the journey itself is braided with a history and cultural significance of the pogo stick.

I exaggerate but the problem is that travel writing, a form of writing about departures, about leaving the known in order to venture into the unknown, could become a stay-at-home genre. Any successful travel book should involve some kind of departure from previously visited ideas of the travel book. Claudio Magris's *Danube* was a subtle expansion of the possibilities of travel writing. Or one could just delete the 'travel' part altogether and say it's a great piece of writing. That deletion cannot always be safely made since certain titles enjoy a reputation as 'travel' classics while falling way below more general standards of literary achievement. Patrick Leigh Fermor's *A Time of Gifts* depends on these standards being dispensed with entirely. (That *would* be an interesting journey: an investigation into the way certain books serve as fake passports, permitting the author to travel to literary immortality without the let or hindrance of critical questioning.)

The 'travel' books I most admire are either much more than travel books or could be classified as something else entirely. To call Rebecca West's *Black Lamb and Grey Falcon*, Ryszard Kapuściński's *The Soccer War* or Don DeLillo's *The Names* (a novel!) 'travel' books is like referring to Miles Davis's music from the 1970s as 'jazz'. For a while, starting with *Filles De Kilimanjaro* (1968), Miles offered his albums as 'Directions in Music'. That's what I'm after: Directions in Writing.

Finally, we might ask: what kinds of writing *aren't* travel writing? We read – often while sitting on a form of mass transit – in order to be privately transported. Geographical distance has nothing to do with it. You can be transported while reading about London on the Tube. Charles Dickens, Annie Dillard, Isak Dinesen and Emily Dickinson (how many writers have taken us to weirder places?) are all travel writers. It's quite natural, therefore – if we may be permitted a couple of alphabetical steps backwards – that E.M. Cioran, of all people, expressed his adoration of Emily Brontë in the form of destination and pilgrimage: 'Haworth is my Mecca'. So the question, to revert to our initial point of departure, becomes: 'Is literature dead?' Answers on a postcard please. ∎

What was travel writing? A testament to the heroic curiosity of the Western spirit: its readiness to dance and drink with the remotest beings, its ability to teach others their own history – and, of course, its uniquely profound sensitivity to human tragedy.

Once upon a time, this meant something. There was actually some truth to the West's universality: Western erudition could be a hard-won gift to the world, and the troubled conscience of Western travellers was sometimes more than just self-discovery.

But it is largely irrelevant today.

In the years since Paul Theroux's classic *The Great Railway Bazaar* (1975), travel itself (in the blithe and expansive sense) has been prohibited to most people on the planet – even as money and those who administer it have become dizzyingly mobile. Since the readers and writers of travel literature are concentrated in those secluded and gated areas of the world whose very viability now depends upon this prohibition, the genre must eventually wither into an aloof kind of reverie. Courtly or besieged, depending on how you look at it.

One and a half million people bought *The Great Railway Bazaar* when it came out – an astounding impact for one person's journey. In today's world, however, 65 million refugees have embarked on their own journeys to escape the violent fallout of our collapsing nation-state system. These journeys are now the real story – and electronic passports are a positive encumbrance to its telling.

Refugees – this roving one per cent of our species – generate a lot of text. Travel literature, written on cracked phones and sent via intermittent Wi-Fi – and in these stuttering chronicles the world is not a sentimental object of contemplation. This is a literature of checkpoints and fences, and the improvised gaps through which desperate people pass. It is a literature of essential tools and documents, and leaving one's soul behind. It is the literature of a world in which the conditions necessary for life are aggressively hoarded, and the real knowledge is not in poetry but survival.

In 'The Storyteller', Walter Benjamin distinguished two equally eternal archetypes of the storyteller: the resident tiller of the soil, and the trading seaman. 'When someone goes on a trip, he has something to tell about,' he wrote, referring to the latter kind.

Travel literature will always be with us. But the centre of experience also shifts in the world. Stupendous traditions end accordingly, and spring up again from new, improbable sources. ■

HIGHER GROUND

Carl De Keyzer

In this series of pictures, taken in Austria, Switzerland, Germany, France and Spain, Belgian photographer Carl De Keyzer has imagined that Europe has flooded and that people have had to move to higher ground to escape the water that has taken over their cities and towns. It's a fantastical thought-experiment made all the more uncanny by the placid and carefree atmosphere of the photographs. The subjects appear to be on holiday: reading and sunbathing by lakes; taking selfies amid stunning scenery; looking out over magnificent vistas through plate-glass windows. In real life, of course, they probably are on holiday. But in the fictional world that De Keyzer has created, these idyllic scenes are unnerving. Despite the evidence on the ground – the melting ice caps, the unusual storms and droughts, the warming world – our complacency about climate change by and large remains intact. These photographs capture that fatal boredom in the face of this slow-motion catastrophe. ∎

A s a child growing up in the seventies in the United States, I learned about European exploration, the 'discovery' of the 'New World' and circumnavigation of the globe. The thrill of treasure, whole parts of the Earth you could claim for yourself, fabled streets of gold and fountains of youth – these were fantastic myths unfolding in my imagination. What I didn't know in fourth grade (when I wrote, directed and starred in a recreation of Columbus 'discovering' the 'New World') was that these were stories of untold violence: murder, rape, enslavement, thievery and the enactment of racist ideologies for the exploitation of black and brown people that continues today.

By the age of two, I had circumnavigated half the globe. I left with my newly married parents aboard a plane from Saigon. Our first stop was the once Kingdom of Hawaii. I didn't know about any of that then either. My 'discovery' was the hotel ice-cube maker and the joy of chewing ice. If it were possible, at age two, I could have written about my discovery of the Hawaiian Islands and their magic machines that made mounds of square frozen water.

We were refugees and yet we were not refugees. My (European American) father worked for the US Department of State; we made our home in the DC area where I learned the Pledge of Allegiance, lived in a brick 'rambler' built for returning World War II vets in the late forties, and learned never to speak Vietnamese. Vietnamese were 'dirty kneed', enemies, a source of guilt or sin.

My Vietnamese mother was born in the Year of the Snake. She left her skin behind and never returned to Vietnam. Like many immigrants, we melted our identities, and yet did not.

*

Growing up, I watched the ease of my white friends, seeing how they could take on the costumes of any era and place: 1950s poodle skirts, elegant saris, beaded 'Indian' tassel-fringed leather outfits, antebellum petticoats. I didn't have the language for why I could not be a tourist in the same way as my white counterparts. I could dress myself as a boy before I could wear period European apparel or the traditional clothing of another nation. And even then it invoked a sense of repulsion and disgust.

Likewise, I'm led to wonder, given the history of 'discovery', if we need more accounts of people of European descent 'discovering' places like my mother's country, my place of birth from which I have felt forever exiled through rupture and circumstance? Do we need more Westerners consuming their way across Vietnam, commenting on local dress, smiles, food and sharing tips on where to get the best deal on bespoke silk skirts?

What is the tourist trade really funding? Is it adult Disneyland, plastic trinkets with little automatons singing 'It's a Small World After All'?

Instead of finding a Western angle of experience in countries like Vietnam – motorbiking from Hanoi to Saigon, boating in the southern delta, snapping up fabric arts from the Hmong, eating their way down the Mekong, seeking redemption from war experiences or war protests, romanticizing French colonialism, or tracing the ghost of writer Marguerite Duras – maybe writers should stick closer to home. What would it look like to travel to a mall, a local wood, a suburban tract – to deeply study and visit one's own locale? As a poet interested in the local, I think it vital to understand what is right before one.

Instead of more consumerism – the buying of experiences, the accumulation of things, of eating the 'other' – perhaps writers should name their own environment. What is the shape of your watershed? How is your electricity produced? Where is your water treated? Where is your food produced and by whom and how does it travel to your local market? What are the names of the rocks under your feet and around you? What formed those geological features? Who were the first humans here? What flora and fauna live upon it and what are their habits and interfaces? What stars whirl above you and what names have they been given, what lore? How can one trace the relations, find the slippages between histories, the linkages, to find the complexities in naming and of the named? Travel as one's carbon footprint; travel as a footstep, travel as a naming in a landscape in all its complexity. Homing as a way to place oneself in a constellation of process and being. ■

Safiya Sinclair

Hymen Elegy

Disobeyed. Sucked the blooded marrow dark, unhooded
    its martyr, wildflower effusing with such
headless agency. Stripped blind my one eye, mutable as the dream

before a storm. Cursed the sterile sky. Cursed the rapeseed
    that fathered you, unfathered me, cursed myself.
Appraised as a trinket, I gave a cowrie shell away. Sold

first to the adulterer, then hawked to shoeless Adam, peddled
    to schoolboys on the country bus. Scratched the demigod
who stole it, dressed as a Judas steer, red moon bellowing. Hot
      nostril-steam

down my back. Dammed my wet scream around those verbs
    for a violence. But I am all teeth. I did not snitch. Went braless
like a bad bitch, horned slick, turned sacral, crotched gold in my wife-

beater and asked for it. Bless my vanity. My charity. How like a parted
    urchin she fills and fills with rheum. Made a killing,
like our language, of the woman I had pilloried. *What a sight*

prized the white man pushing his Mag-Lite into it, a game to see
    just where a girl like me could go. *So tight* he whispered
from beyond the haze, thrusting until she was no longer a part of me,

undone under world, pressed full and unfathomed, pulped raw
    as a meathole. O plastic. O raggedy-ann. This is what you wanted.
Ripped button for eyes and yarn for hair; she will not grow nor come

alive. How widening loneliness is a gift again. First opening
    greedy on that Christmas bulb, flush, lit-up. Half-angel.
The old ghost, unfondling on his tender threat, will never knock me up,

The trope of the encounter with the other is really, at its heart, an encounter with oneself.

In our selfie culture, in which even ISIS members glower at their camera phones and snap their own portraits, the fascination with the story of oneself has never been more tantalising.

Take for instance the tourist I spied not long ago at Café Les Deux Magots filming her magenta macaroon for Snapchat, or its ilk. (I didn't ask. I'm making an assumption for the purposes of argument, the cardinal right of the travel writer.)

At the next table, another young girl fondled and photographed her dessert for her Instagram. (You, dear reader, will have to wonder if I'm now creating this second character to make my point. This isn't fact-checkable – another weapon of the far-flung correspondent, even if it's only Paris.)

The point is, did one young woman's delectation render the other's any less compelling a journey? When each returned late that evening to her tiny slope-ceilinged garret to draft her respective dispatch on social media, did the fact that someone across town was doing exactly the same thing invalidate her adventure?

Of course not.

Although it's certainly true that we no longer need travel writing to bring us to unknown places, the question is: were we reading these narratives solely to learn about place? I'd argue not. I'd argue we were reading a report on the state of the writer's consciousness. We were reading for interest and pleasure, perhaps a spinal shiver if the place involved risk, but primarily we read for the self, not the other.

And now I must out myself. After all, what was I doing in Café Les Deux Magots but on a trip to Paris designed to shift my consciousness. I was, I was, trying to write a poem. Ick! Blech! An embarrassing revelation, but nonetheless, I'd just consumed two pots – not *tasses* – of hot chocolate in order to sit there with my notebook, like every other American whose loud yammer clattered off the tiled floors. I saw myself as so different, so deserving of the place! What a tender farce! There we all were, trying to imagine ourselves as special – as better than we were. I was trying to manufacture a space in which I might imagine myself capable of filling the blank page before me in a startling way.

Even in its subtler forms, the act of looking is an act of self-regard. ■

Zeyar Lynn

Nobody Represents Me

You & I sit on a bench that goes nowhere
We stare at the wall
If we can afford the agent fee, we can go to Malaysia, Korea, Dubai,
    Saudi
Gotta do what we gotta do
Blood circulation is no entertainment
Like ice cream in green tea
Like winning an eye from a mosquito coil, lucky draw
Dig your own well & drink your own limestone water
Must be fate that gave you a life well demarcated to an inch
In a brand new satellite town far away from the city centre
The sun goes out in the morning, returns in the evening, as is its nature
What courses have you attended in plastic standard time? What
    certificates?
Roadside bowl of boiled beef guts
MADE IN JAPAN Chinese wristwatch
There's a war going on in Afghanistan
There's an election going on in Afghanistan
The singer sings, the player plays, the dancer dances, I am a mason
What shall I do? Is it inappropriate to express my feelings?
Family well sinks lower & lower but not to worry keep my chin up
Yo bro, we both live in a brand new satellite town
You got bus fare? Let's go occupy the city for a few hours
We must be poetry because we have no utilitarian value
So dumb we don't know how to generate electricity by blocking an
    artery
Ecology of ethics too is warming up, my friend
Construction worker? Corpse cleaner? Singapore? Japan?

Do I have the heart to drink a glass of cool Coke?
Have to learn, get an education, increase knowledge, & so on & so
    forth
Hey, look. One comes out of the interview room. Hand gestures failure
What about me? Can I afford to pay tea money?
Is that guy's pocket fatter than mine?
I look at my docile hands that know nothing else
Sing dollar? Malay ringgit? Thai baht? Japanese yen?
Burmese kyats & pyas?
The stench of the cubicle in the unclean public toilet
Life is so wholesome I say & wait for my name to be called out
You & I we sit face-to-face on a train
Our duty is to change the scenery by turns
In order to go out, I soak my value in water to soften it
If wife were to ask where I had been the whole day
& I replied, 'Nowhere,' would she believe me?
The world has become flat, they say
We are round objects precisely timed.

Translated from the Burmese by the author

Taj Hotel, Mumbai, November 2008

FRIEND OF MY YOUTH

Amit Chaudhuri

'We have long forgotten the ritual by which the house of our life
was erected. But when it is under assault and enemy bombs are
already taking their toll, what enervated, perverse antiquities do
they not lay bare in the foundations. What things were interred
and sacrificed amid magic incantations, what horrible cabinet of
curiosities lies there below, where the deepest shafts are reserved
for what is most commonplace. In a night of despair I dreamed
I was with my first friend from my school days, whom I had not
seen for decades and had scarcely ever remembered in that time,
tempestuously renewing our friendship and brotherhood. But
when I awoke it became clear that what despair had brought to
light like a detonation was the corpse of that boy, who had been
immured as a warning: that whoever one day lives here may in no
respect resemble him.'
– Walter Benjamin

I think of Ramu when I read these lines. It's of him I think when
I reread them. I have no idea why. For one thing, Ramu isn't 'my
first friend from my school days' – though he's the only surviving
school friend I'll see when I visit Bombay. Bombay: the city I grew up

in. The city I grew up in but knew very little. That is, a pretty limited number of roads; specific clusters of buildings.

I feel a deep sadness reading these lines – I can't say why.

When I arrive into Bombay, I make phone calls. This is in the taxi, or the car that's come to receive me from the airport and take me to wherever it is I'm staying: club or hotel. All the while, I'm registering the unfamiliar: the new flyovers; the disappearance of certain things which weren't quite landmarks but which helped you orient yourself – furniture showrooms; fisherfolk's settlements. I would be surprised – maybe even disappointed – if these large-scale changes did *not* occur. On the right-hand side at the end of the road from the airport towards Mahim is, I know, the mosque with loudspeakers, hemmed in by traffic; on the left, further up, past the brief stink of the sea, will be the church where I once went to attend an NA meeting. I was keeping Ramu company. These aren't parts in which I grew up – but my childhood is coming back to me: the terror – the bewilderment and impatience. The contempt for others. For the city. The magical sense of superiority – like an armour – nurtured inadvertently by your parents: hard to regain.

This is a new route. It's very grandiose.

A bridge suspended over water. I've been on it twice before. It is still. In the monsoons, its cables look immovable against the sheets of rain. Suddenly there's an island, low and humped, with irregular houses and a temple, which you never saw on the old route (that route's roughly parallel to this one, which is seaborne). Fisherfolk. No slum. The original islanders – you can't but romanticise them when granted such a glimpse. They were invisible – perhaps for more than a century – from the Mahim side. Maybe they preferred it that way. Maybe they never realised they were invisible. Maybe they don't know they're visible. Of course, they'd have noticed the bridge come up over the years. Children would have grown up and left in the time. Do they leave? It doesn't look like a place to go away from. The houses have a light wash – pale yellow, or pink, or white.

The bridge doesn't last long – it's meant to cut the duration of the journey. When you're on it, you want it – the straight lines, the geometry, the inviolable sterility – to last longer. There are no pedestrians. Everything you claim to miss – human noise, congestion – you cease to miss when you're on the bridge. Death in life. The other end dumps the cars into Worli. The wrong side of Worli. The car needs to make a U-turn round the potholes. In place of the old sea-facing bungalows, the high buildings for the new rich flank the left. The sea on the right is desolate, though it isn't next to Marine Drive or before the Gateway or even in Juhu. Your first taste of the sea: contained, menacing. Contrary to your desires, you've been deposited in the middle of nowhere – which is what Worli was, and is. Still, the signal has come back – you can make calls again.

Instead, I send out a smarmy text to two acquaintances. 'I'll be doing a reading on the 5th at 6.30 p.m. at . . . And performing on the 6th at 8 p.m. Do come if you're free.' This silly message, bound for people I hardly know, flies out of my mobile as the car turns right towards Haji Ali. I detest messaging. Any variety of need leads to unease. But I mustn't take the audience for granted.

'Aaj kal mausam kaisa hai?' I ask the driver – the weather's the best subject when you've just released a text and are about to get bored.

At my request, he's turned down the volume of his CD player, which has been broadcasting lushly arranged covers of film songs by a mediocre singer – why covers rather than the originals I don't know, because the latter are easier to procure. Could, maybe, the singer be *him*? People believe in multitasking in Bombay. It's a word used frequently here.

'Garmi shuru ho gayi hai,' he says, sombre, matter-of-fact. It's March; no vestiges of coolness. Anyway, Bombay has no winter. Everyone knows that, but I get a sense that he thinks I might not know. He's a true-blue 'Mumbaikar'; I'm a tourist – he tests my knowledge by gently asking me my route preferences. He has no idea I grew up here – I, a man collected from the airport – that this city was long ago my life. I'm tempted to share this information, but have no opportunity. Instead, every time the car stops at a light, I stare at the vendors of pirated books who magically appear, who assess you with a piercing gaze as they brandish Jhumpa Lahiri; and the dark girls selling unblemished mogra flowers. White bracelets. 'Bisnes pe aya?' he asks me. I suppose writing is a business. Yes, I'm here on business. But I don't tell him what kind, because I presume he won't understand. What am I up to? If I made millions and entertained millions, there would be a justification; but . . . Nevertheless, I am here, and people, oddly, accept me for what I do. Even the driver would probably be okay with it. Now, the word 'business' – it has such a malleability in the language. 'The business of writing a poem.'

I feel a sense of purposelessness – is it the ennui of the book tour or book-related visit? Not entirely. No, it pertains to Bombay, to being returned to a city where one performed a function, reluctantly. Reluctance is fundamental. You don't plunge into growing up; it happens in spite of you. Then, one day, it's done: you're 'grown up'. You go away. Back now in the city of my growing up, there's nothing more that can happen to me. I embrace a false busyness. I suppose I'm living life. Without necessarily meaning to. It doesn't occur to me that the visit is part of my life. I believe I'll *resume* life after it's done.

Ramu. Now, I don't spectate on him as I do on the city: as a relic of my boyhood. My oldest surviving friend in Bombay. That makes it sound like the other friends are dead. But you know what I mean. We argue a lot: it's not unequivocal affection. He's irritating. I have delusions of grandeur. But we're both reliable.

Ramu isn't in Bombay. He's in rehab in Alibagh. It sounds like a punitive regime: you can't talk to him on the phone. He cannot leave. His sister gives me his news: not that there's any news. She says he went in voluntarily. The regime will cure him once and for all of – what was it? It used to be 'brown sugar'; is that still the fix? The stuff has become 'shit', Ramu once told me. Horribly impure. He's been in Alibagh for a year; he'll be in there for another. Unbelievable! But prevarication was possible no more. He'd come close to death once (I was here at the time) on his first and only overdose (he's a chronic but doubtful user; he flirts with but doesn't revel in danger; he's timid). He lived, courtesy of the kindness of an extraordinary policeman. And a doctor called Shailendra. He lived; he was convinced he'd had some sense knocked into him. He had a certain look on his face for a year. Like a hare that's felt the velocity of a bullet passing a centimetre from its ear. Then, slowly, he became himself. 'How do I look? How do I look?' he asked, narrowing his eyes – he's always keen to know how others see him. And he's also completely indifferent to opinion – a curious paradox. 'You're looking yourself again,' I lied. He had aged, lost some hair and put on weight. Epitome of middle-class anonymity; he even wore terecot trousers, not jeans. But the self-absorbed expression was back. I was relieved as well as concerned. After a year, he 'slipped' again. He disappeared into the rehab without telling me; I don't know when. I call him very occasionally, when seized by duty or a faint nostalgia. We have nothing really to say to each other, except the usual – his health, drugs, life, Bombay, what he might achieve if he were gainfully employed, masturbation, the girls we knew in school. He makes some cursory but sincere enquiries after my family. He's fond of my parents.

The truth is: I've always expected to see him again, whether or not I *wanted* to. I haven't assigned it priority. It's a given. I'll phone him and go to his place when I'm bored in the afternoons. He'll turn up at the hotel I'm staying at, or at the Bombay Gymkhana; I'll sign for him in the visitors book. Or he'll come to the venue where I'm reading at half an hour before the event begins; he'll sit stoically in the audience. Although he's dismissive and impatient, he's quite capable of fortitude. In the evenings, I'll take him out to a dinner or two, sometimes in company, comprising other writers, which makes him restive, and confirms his worst prejudice about 'intellectuals'. I draw the line at times: tell him I can't see him when I have interviews and meetings. I wonder if this makes the relationship exploitative. It's a question submerged at the back of my mind. But it's okay to want friends to be available, right?

Lacan says our subjectivity takes form at the 'mirror stage'. The term and notion are so well worn they might make you laugh – the fate of most revolutionary ideas in psychoanalysis. At around the age of one, we apparently begin to recognise ourselves in the mirror. That tottering toddler is *me*. Lacan points out that our relationship with our image is partly libidinous. Naturally, I have no memory of first noticing myself in a glass; but I do recall viewing myself pruriently even when I was four or five – making of my twin my sexual playmate, lingering over him. Handloom House on Dadabhai Naoroji Road – the place went up in a fire in the eighties. I remember pressing against my reflection as my mother pored over saris.

There must be other leaps in life – as momentous as the 'mirror stage' – that Lacan didn't mention. Some are universal; others, culturally particular. To understand that your parents are human (and not an element of the natural world), that they're separate from you, that they were children once, that they were born and came into the world, is another leap. It's as if you hadn't seen who they were earlier – just as, before you were ten months old, you didn't know it was you in the mirror. This happens when you're sixteen or seventeen. Not long after – maybe a year – you find out your parents will die. It's not as if you haven't encountered death already. But, before now, your precocious mind can't accommodate your parents' death except as an academic nicety – to be dismissed gently as too literary and sentimental. After that day, your parents' dying suddenly becomes simple. It grows clear that you're alone and always have been, though certain convergences start to look miraculous – for instance, between your father, mother and yourself. Though your parents don't die immediately – what you've had is a realisation, not a premonition – you'll carry around this knowledge for their remaining decades or years. You won't think, looking at them, 'You're going to die.' It'll be an unspoken fact of existence. Nothing about them will surprise you any more. My awareness of this fact is never far away on this trip.

Ramu's absence – it's thrown me off balance and taken me aback a bit. I wonder how to categorise it. Which stage could it be part of? The mirror stage; the stage at which you realise what it means that your parents will die; the stage at which you realise your friends will not be permanently there – is the last a recognised stage?

D iagonally across the Kamala Nehru Park is the club. The taxi turns left; this is my destination. The main entrance – I lift my bag up three steps. Actually, the main entrance isn't the right one for guests about to occupy a room. You have to walk down the long veranda (again, on your left) to the reception at the other end to collect your key. Something's going to happen in the evening: PARSI NITE WITH BUFFET AND PERCY KHAMBATTA ON THE ACCORDION.

There's a long sofa here, before which the broadsheets are placed on a table. To these are added, later, the tabloid-sized afternoon papers.

Each time I arrive here, I remember. This is where we came – my parents and I – when we left Bombay. I was in Oxford then. But I'd returned on one of my many homecomings and joined forces with my parents in the move. When I say 'left', I don't mean we were going on holiday, though I behaved as if we were. We were making our exit. I didn't care: it happened as simply as sloughing off a skin. My parents would be gone, elsewhere – to Calcutta. We had finished our life here, snipped off formal ties. I claimed never to love Bombay. I was making, with my parents, a long-awaited egress. Tired, we came to this club, to spend the last two nights here. My father's flat had been sold; we had no home now in Bombay. The club became a second home – my father was a life member. We were tired but – probably – satisfied, that the money and the property had changed hands. My mother sat down on the sofa before which the broadsheets are kept. Was the reception then on this side, near the main entrance? I recall being visited by a sense of déjà vu on entering the club. I was often getting déjà vu then; I'd felt it when I saw all our possessions – books, furniture, china – being put inside crates. Then, in the club's lobby, I had the faintest of memories: I had *dreamed* of the crates earlier, I'd also dreamed of arriving one afternoon in the club with my parents. This gave me a slight chill: so what I'd had was a premonition of our departure, and the déjà vu was not déjà vu at all, it was the feeling of experiencing what had been foretold in the dreams I'd had those days, when my parents lived in Bandra and were thinking of departing, and I would return to them in their unresolved state every three or four months. I half smile as this comes back to me.

I nod at the man and the woman who pilot the reception desk. 'How are you?' 'Fine, sir! Your father is okay?' 'He's all right, thank you!' They sway their heads from side to side, denoting satisfaction and closure – more a doll-like vibration than a head movement. They ask after my father because he's the member, not I. Where *is* he? The man behind the desk is warmly deferential, the woman is businesslike – the club's female staff aren't unduly forthcoming. I walk past PERCY KHAMBATTA ON THE ACCORDION (wondering if I should slip into Parsi Nite in the evening: I have a weakness for Parsi food) and turn left into the corridor where members are sitting in a cluster of limbs: arms, legs, tennis rackets. Parsis and Gujaratis: a breezy, gregarious bunch. But also oddly clannish. The staff emanate from Deccan soil. When Datta Samant was the guru of the trade unions in the seventies, this club, like every other, was rife with labour–employer warfare. Only part of the tension has to do with class: there's also race and community. The affluent émigrés; the deprived natives. Right now, no one seems to be in a mood to move: the waiters stand in gossipy circles; the members lean towards tables or raise eyes and throw questions at each other.

I remember when this club was nothing: an underpopulated building, a government canteen. On Sundays, you'd see three or four members being served rice from a big china bowl, alongside Goa fish curry and kachumber. The kitchen was, and is, out of sight; the food and the waiter carrying it on a tray had covered great distances.

It's 1970 I'm thinking of. That's when we moved to the tall building, Toledo, that had come up behind the club. Each resident of Toledo – as my father was from 1970 – was given life membership of the club: probably to both increase and improve its clientele. Just as well, because it meant we could use the club as a pied-à-terre or whatever the right term is when we left Bombay, and have been able to continue to use it in that way ever since. It has changed greatly. Its location in the richest area in the city and the fact that it has no special colonial pedigree mean it's both attractive to potential members and less difficult to join (provided you have the money) than the older clubs (which, it's rumoured, take no new members). You must keep this in mind as you walk past the people sunk languorously in the cavities of chairs and sofas. They may not be the crème de la crème, but they are rich. Anyway, who's to decide who constitutes the old rich, or if that category is even pertinent here? On certain visits, when I step into the main entrance in the evenings and overhear the din, I'm reminded of Noam Chomsky's incredulous assertion: 'No one parties as much as the Indian upper classes do.' The club has changed again, but that's to do with readjusting the veneer every year: adding granite, changing the name of a restaurant. The core clientele remains the same; so does the core of the menu: sev puri, chutney sandwich, dhansak, Parsi chutney. When you ask for coffee, there are two options: 'Nescafé', a mound of instant-coffee powder in a jar alongside the hot water, or 'filter coffee', a species of south Indian granule that you spot on the bottom of the cup, beneath the swill, or taste as a sediment. If you order tea, the waiter will ask if you like it 'mixed', with water, leaves, milk and sugar amalgamated into a potion, or 'separate'. I usually opt for 'separate'.

I lie back. They've 'refurbished' the room. I loathe the word, its blunt sound (as if someone with a cold were trying to say 'furnished'), and don't use it without irony. But the room is new. Oddly, it's erased the old room from my memory – all I recall is the bathroom, and the plastic bucket that was left under the shower for good measure.

I close my eyes. The air conditioning is fixed at twenty-three degrees centigrade – although there's a remote control on the bedside table, it's symbolic; you can make no alteration to the temperature. Why didn't I accept my hosts' invitation to stay in a new boutique hotel in Apollo Bunder? Perhaps it was the temptation to be an interloper – to spend a few nights, not by proxy but by stealth, in Little Gibbs Road: our address when I was a boy. Close, but not too close. Just to be able to catch a heartbeat. And make my getaway. The refurbished room, with its new bed, prints, mirror and unfluctuating weather, is more expensive than the old version – but absurdly affordable. I'll claim the expenses, of course. We writers might not earn much by way of fees, but every part of our trip is covered. On tour, we are on loan. We're the pound of flesh that must be repaid in full.

With nothing to do, with Ramu absent, I go down for a walk. Arjun is missing too; he's flown to Delhi to give a talk on the gene. I met him when we were in Oxford. He now runs a government-funded lab on the outskirts of Bombay. He's one of those who, like me, made the decision to return to India. Like me, he couldn't stand the idea of living in the West a single day longer. Unlike me, Arjun hasn't stepped out of India since 1998 – although he's planning to accept an invitation to a conference in Birmingham. I wonder at his tardiness. When we meet up, we rarely discuss matters of weight; we mostly talk like we were teenagers, or unmarried – as we used to in Oxford. Ramu is suspicious of our candour. He has deemed Arjun an 'intellectual'; the one concession he'll make is, 'He's nice, but horny.' The 'but' is interesting. It contains Ramu's sense of moral superiority. He has many occasions to declare he's morally superior – as an addict, cheated by the city he grew up in; as a non-intellectual; as one who's less horny than Arjun. But, whenever he carps gently about Arjun, I participate in Ramu's generalisations and implicitly agree. Yes, we *are* less horny than him.

I emerge from the gates of the club onto the main road and glance to my left at Kamala Nehru Park. I feel no time lag. I catch sight of the park as I used to each day as a boy. Another part of me, hovering a few feet overhead, is studying my situation. Because this is not my life. It could have been, but I chose for it not to be. Instead of turning left, I turn right, deciding to shop. Unzipping my toilet bag in the room, I noticed I'd left the toothpaste behind. So I enter the provisions store. I used to get index-finger-sized Cadbury's milk chocolate bars here; they cost a rupee when I was eight years old. I used to love the fact that the bar was so thin and lapidary and would be gone in ten seconds. I barely felt responsible for being the cause of its disappearance. I loved the lettering and sinking my teeth into it. Now, I go up the two steps and find the shop is as busy as if it were Christmas. The Gujaratis within are amenable – they furnish me with Colgate in fifteen seconds. I pay, and consider buying something else – one of the staff is perched on a ladder to retrieve a lotion from the topmost shelf. Everywhere, there is the strain and stretch of trade.

It's a wonder the shop exists. Could it be here because there's such affluence in Malabar Hill – or is it here despite the wealth? The same could be said of the shops next to it: St Stephen's Store on its right, a confectioner's, and the two grocers' on its left. I first saw them more than four decades ago. Why do the rich give them patronage? Could it be that they want tiny pockets of continuity? Actually, Malabar Hill is an oasis of continuity – its tranquillity is calculated to preserve. When I lived here, I never went into these shops except the one from which I've acquired toothpaste – to get my Cadbury's, or watch my mother buy a tin of Kraft cheese. It's only now, when I've become a visitor, that I've discovered St Stephen's Store, and its tissue-thin chutney sandwiches. There are certain things that (obeying orders) I buy for my family when I'm in Bombay, and one or two that I give myself, such as these sandwiches. They're part of my afterlife here.

I cross the road. I'm here for the book reading; I've nothing to do this afternoon – or later this evening. I didn't have the wit to notify my friends in advance. But, then, I don't have friends here. The idea is a fiction that I hardly ever bother to examine – which is why I'm often taken by surprise when I find myself at a loose end in Bombay. My mind tells me, 'Bombay is teeming with people you know, or have known.' This doesn't stand up to scrutiny. The people I was close to in school I've lost track of. Except Ramu.

I have crossed the road. Opposite me is the building that came up out of nowhere in the late seventies and partially blocked our view. Before then, we had an unbroken vision of the Arabian Sea. The building is irrelevant to me now, but still causes a pinprick of irritation. It was an interloper – a tenant on the landscape – and continues to be one.

In front of the building, upon the road – there's no pavement here – sits a woman on her haunches, displaying a basket of fruit. What she could offer that the grocers opposite don't, I can't say. In another area, there'd be a gaggle of squatting women. Here, she is one. One is enough for Little Gibbs Road.

Next to her there's a narrow pathway or steps that fall precipitately seaward. Itinerants descend. I catch a blue glimpse of the horizon. I have never been down there. That's because we've spent so much of our lives, even in places we've grown up in, being driven around. Walking, we take expected routes. Even our unexpected routes are well worn. There's much I don't know in Malabar Hill. Like that glimpse of blue.

I feel no nostalgia. What I confront is an impossibility – of recovering whatever it was that formed me, which I churlishly disowned. Bombay was never good enough for me. Even now – as before – I hesitate to write about it. It is my secret. It was so, even when I lived here. For instance, the Mercedes. My father's white Mercedes-Benz, 'Merc' to my friends. 'Mercheditch' to the proud driver. I rode it but disembarked ten minutes before reaching Elphinstone College. The final bit I covered on foot. Sloughing off my life. And no sooner has the thought suggested itself than I confront the bus terminus near the Kamala Nehru Park. From here ply the 102 and the 106. Red double-decker and single-decker respectively. Sturdy carriers

– not like their derelict Calcutta counterparts. With the Mercedes presenting itself and escape from it becoming a necessity, I began for the first time to take buses. Incredible cocoon they took me out of. The 106 put me in the middle of the sea breeze and dropped me close to Elphinstone College. Sometimes, I lugged my guitar along. Fittingly, my hair would be insanely tousled by the time I arrived.

The *Immortals* is my fifth novel. It's also my longest one. On paper, it took me nine years to write, but the duration is misleading. I didn't spend all of it writing my new novel. It would have been interesting to have had some sort of a timekeeper who could have measured the moments I spent writing it. Maybe the total of a year devoted to committing the actual story to the page? Even that seems an excessive span, a phantasmagoric labour. One year! No, I was plotting other things at the time – plotting not the novel, but that resistant tale we call 'life'. At the very end of the millennium, I tried to escape globalisation by escaping Britain. I didn't want to go back to a time *before* globalisation; I just wanted to get out, move. I moved to Calcutta. Then I tried to escape globalisation by taking leave of the novel. I wrote stories. I wrote essays. I composed music. This is what I did a lot of those nine years.

I am in the Kamala Nehru Park. I've entered through the open gates. I love the Kamala Nehru Park, but I didn't frequent it as a child. It served as a landmark: 'We live near Kamala Nehru Park.' Even today, I will – if I'm staying at the club – instruct the taxi driver: 'It's opposite the Kamala Nehru Park.' Because everyone seems to know it. I love it, but my discovery of it goes back to a reassessment made in my late teens. I began to explore certain things I'd ignored till then, and which had always been close at hand. Among these were Indian classical music, black-and-white Hindi films, Hindi film songs – and even a place like the Kamala Nehru Park. I can't pinpoint what connects these things I've mentioned except that they'd always been in front of me – but I'd never noticed them. They weren't on the curriculum of my upper-middle-class life. By the time I was sixteen or seventeen, the outline of that life was loosening, it was being tugged at its edges. I was making those discoveries largely alone.

The Kamala Nehru Park's clientele – in fact, Indian tourism – is predominantly working class. We think the working class spends all its time working; actually, recreation is an avid pursuit for wage earners and 'blue collar' workers. They come from faraway localities (Ghatkopar, Mulund) – possibly taking the 106 on the last leg of the expedition. They arrive as families; male friends roam the park in pairs – holding hands: this much hasn't changed. You can spot the upper-middle-class person native to this area because the men are in shorts and the women wear trainers. You see them running; one marches past briskly. They return in your direction in seven minutes. The upper-middle-class person is an individual; they don't circulate in the park in groups. The visitors from Mulund hardly run; their progress is deliberate. The man of the family is regal in his patience. A family might loll on the grass with a familiarity that resembles ownership. The children run. They rush to the circular raised platform, whose roof beats and vibrates during the monsoons. When a child stamps his foot, there's an answering echo, like a swift, painless slap, special to the podium. All this is as I recall from a year ago, and from forty years ago too. This isn't to say that Bombay is unchanged – Bombay, least changeless of cities! But a few things – like the loud echo here – *are* the same as ever; annunciatory; to be encountered nowhere else.

I like it when I get invitations to read in Bombay – or to give a talk here. Especially as I get so few. No one wants me to read in Bombay. That's an exaggeration. I'm not being singled out. It's just that literary events here are few and far between. It's more likely that I'll get an invitation tomorrow from Abu Dhabi, or Barcelona, or Rangoon. The city belongs to Bollywood. That's what constitutes its imaginative energy, its drive. It has no academia to speak of; its university has been made peripheral. And that's why I await the invitation or opportunity – for months, sometimes for a year – with a strange anticipation. It's not that I want to disseminate my work in Bombay. It's just that I long, these days, to visit the city I grew up in.

And who'll come to the reading? I can predict the mix. There might be one or two people whose names I guess at vaguely, but there will be few faces from the past. Few friends from school; few colleagues of my father's. And yet there's a recognisability about the audience – I know them, their clothes and accent. What brings them to my reading? I'm not confident they know me. I'm used to being no one in Bombay – I've experienced years and years of anonymity here, or, more accurately, being an extension of my father's identity. Mr Chaudhuri's son. As was the case at the club earlier. 'How's your dad?' It's a question I'm used to in Bombay.

The park diagonally opposite the Kamala Nehru is called the Hanging Gardens, but it feels to me that the park is the one that hangs over the city. Hanging Gardens is situated on a slight elevation on Malabar Hill; at least, so it seems when you approach it from the club and the Post Office, and climb twenty-odd steps to its gates to find that Hanging Gardens is the top of a plateau. It's more middle class than Kamala Nehru, many more purposeful walkers, their calves bare, socks gathered round ankles. Optimistic foliage sculptures abound: a rhinoceros; a boy on an elephant; a giraffe. These are best ignored. The oddity at the core of the Kamala Nehru Park is the great shoe. The rhyme it solemnly provoked when you first saw it as a child was 'There was an old woman who lived in a shoe', mapping the park in your head according to a list of imaginary habitations, of which that abode made of confectionery (which Hansel and Gretel began to eat bits of the moment they found it) was also one. I've never entered the shoe. It's a storey tall; people are always going up. I go down paths flanked with flowers – there are so many whose names I don't know; I'm no nature lover, the only blossoms I'm familiar with are gulmohur and bougainvillea – till I come to the balcony where the park is a promontory overlooking, all at once, Marine Drive, the eye-hurting glint of the Arabian Sea, bits of Marine Lines, the narrowing at Nariman Point, the clusters of very tall, at times very thin, buildings, the extant Gothic towers and turrets and antiquarian domes, and, across all of this, the sea, which extends beyond the Gateway of India. You'd expect a throng here, at this balcony, but it's a manageable crowd. Families; boys straining; fathers complacent; the mothers harangued. Only the little girls look thrilled. Naturally, no denizen of Bombay would come here; at least, none who felt they belonged to the city or had a sense of proprietorship. Which is why I crane to look but try not to take too much time, so others behind me can occupy my place. It's a magnificent scene, an old, old one, which I'd glimpsed from one spot or another in Malabar Hill since I was a child, blankly, appearing to register little; and now, seeing it again, I don't know what to do with it. And so, almost immediately, I turn my back on Bombay, and am now looking at the children who are buzzing before me, who know there's definitely something at hand.

With Bombay and the oncoming evening behind me – the giant pink wash over the sea is expanding – I walk up the red path to the gates and am back at the bus stop again. There's a short-lived agitation in my pocket; the phone's convulsing. I fish it out. The message says: *Don't forget the shoes.* Of course. Something to do! I might have forgotten. I stare and then write, *Remind me of details. Can't recall.* As I proceed to the club, the phone shivers again. *Just take them. Call when you're there.*

They're furled in the suitcase in the room, my wife's shoes and my mother's. Their bones bulge slightly in the cloth bag. I transfer the cloth bag to a plastic one and exit the room. This is my big mission in Bombay, to exchange these bespoke pairs for my mother and wife; either the fit or the colour wasn't right. My mother, even today, approaching her mid-eighties, will wear no other footwear but Joy Shoes. The shop came up in the Taj in the seventies. She became a customer. She's been unflinching in her loyalty. Even now, when she can no longer travel to Bombay, she'll order a pair over the phone. 'Munna?' she says. 'How are you?' in that rich Bengali-accented diction. Munna's a suave operator. 'Hello madam, hello madam, all well here. When are you coming next this side?' 'I am not coming but my son is going,' says my mother firmly. 'Please exchange the priya you sent me last time, they are not fitting properly.' 'Send it over, send it over,' he responds breezily. 'Anything else?' 'My daughter-in-law . . .' she repeats these important words, '*my daughter-in-law* never wore the kolhapuri she bought last time. Please exchange them for priya.' 'No problem,' says Munna, clearly preoccupied with other things. 'You are size 5, right?' 'Four and a half,' she corrects him. 'My daughter-in-law is six,' she adds, though no request was made for this information. Their feet are small, but my mother's are specially tiny, and probably has Joy Shoes sending specifications to workmen for a new pair of priya. At the end of this conversation, my mother and I (who have known him since I was fourteen) are gratified that Munna is alive, given the strange events of 26/11. A close shave. It's been two years. Still, my mother makes sure: 'You are okay?' 'Oh yes, yes!' says Munna, not guessing the association – he's adept at being reassuring.

The taxi driver will test your knowledge. He's planted his car in front of El Cid. The moment I cross the road and say 'Taj Mahal', he perks up. 'Babulnath se jau ya Walkeshwar se jau?' He knows the query about the route is rhetorical. 'Walkeshwar,' I say, meeting his eyes in the mirror. We're soon past the Jain Temple, whose striking blue pillars I've only seen from the outside, we've turned round the Teen Batti hairpin, left behind the Governor's House, and are suddenly by the sea. I am now *in* the scene I was looking at earlier; it's the one I stared upon morning and evening from the twelfth-floor balcony. The way to school. By the time I was fourteen, I'd have known this journey couldn't be repeated forever. When I was smaller, there was no end in sight to the morning excursion to class. I took to prayer in the car. The praying was furtive. No one knew about it: not my parents; not the driver. Once a girl in a school bus saw me, and I agonised over whether I'd been discovered. I depended on the Catholic figurines that seemed to hide behind every other corner on the route. My prayers asked for exemption from PE. 'Please let Mr Mazumdar not tell me to run today,' I begged – I wasn't certain if the addressee was 'God'. There was always a saint in waiting. In a traffic jam in Marine Lines, I saw a kindly shape that said OUR LADY OF DOLOURS beneath it. I sent the prayer in her direction. This was when, from a neighbouring vantage point above the car window, the girl saw me. I saw her just after I opened my eyes. Why I was in Marine Lines I don't know. Usually the car went up the flyover and then descended into Dhobi Talao, or went to Churchgate and turned left at the IRAN AIR sign.

As we go down Marine Drive, I see a sign proclaiming NIKHIL CHAGANLAL. I'd missed it before now. Unless it's new. It doesn't *look* new. Could this be the Nikhil Chaganlal who teased me mercilessly in the sixth standard? The sign says he's a painter. That night, I google him on my laptop. It *is* him. The face matches. He was a scrawny boy; he's better built now. His 'recent works' include a series on rooms – mainly bedrooms and sitting rooms. There are no human beings in them, but there's evidence of activity. There's a chessboard on the bed; sitar and tablas by the sofa; a can of Coke on the rug, bright red. The colours have an intolerable gaiety. The view from the rooms contains the sea – not quite the Bombay sea (it's too blue). The paintings simmer uniformly, as if on a steady, low flame. I am engrossed. I must have presumed (without realising it) that I'm the only one in that sixth-standard class who's 'famous'. Or at least had artistic ambition.

There's a great bustle outside the Taj. Once it had to do with chauffeurs arrayed there, waiting for the sahebs. Now it's the new security regime. The men who brought death here a little more than two years ago disembarked from a dinghy near Cuffe Parade, and then some of them arrived at Apollo Bunder and got into the lobby with guns. To delay the likes of them in the future, you have to put your packages through the X-ray machine and your mobile in a small coffin-like tray. These Joy shoes of my mother's and my wife's belong, in a sense, as much to the Taj as they do to them. I surrender them to the X-ray tunnel. *Go back to where you came from. Let them accuse you of being dangerous.*

Once inside, I ignore the sofas that, in the centre, form a commoner's court, a Diwan-i-Aim, in which the visitor can be enthroned. This was long the axis of the Taj's new wing. There's something subtly different about the arrangement of the sofas – it's sparser – in comparison to the lot these have replaced and which were presumably destroyed. To the veteran visitor, this loss of continuity is near-unnoticeable; for the new guest, the Taj they see – the busy lobby – is a phoenix risen from the flames. I head for Nalanda. I may as well check if they have a copy of *The Immortals*. The reason for checking is to punish myself. It's not the bookshop it was; besides, its representation of my work is patchy. My visits to Nalanda are coterminous with my trips to Bombay: annual; once in two years. I will ask them straight out, 'Where are my books?', or, if they have one or two allocated to random bookshelves, 'And my other books?' I feel compelled to excavate my titles because I bought books here as a teenager – not just bought books, but lighted on poets I'd never heard of: Tranströmer, then Mandelstam and Pessoa. The irony of a five-star hotel hosting these elusive men concerned neither the bookshop nor me. Once I became aware that Sharmila Tagore (smaller than I expected) was standing beside me, *The Faber Book of Contemporary Stories* in her hand, reading, or – from the resistance she emanated delicately – pretending to read. There's little poetry in Nalanda these days: maybe a Palgrave anthology; Tagore; Kapil Sibal. If you're in luck, you might spot Imtiaz Dharker's *Postcards from God*. To my question, the attendant has an all-purpose comeback: 'We just sold out. We have placed order with distributor, but they are not supplying.' If I were to pin down the publishing rep (he's so intangible he's almost non-existent), he will shake his head and confide (I don't know if he's shaking his head, since we're on the phone, but it feels like he is): 'Nalanda balance of payment is very bad, sir. Long backlog of credit. We have stopped supplying till they clear the deficit.' Sceptical, I say, 'That's terrible, Janardhan. The Taj is an important outlet, right?' 'I agree, sir,' he replies blandly. 'I'm trying to rectify it.' 'Do they even know that I've written about the Taj and Nalanda in *The Immortals*?' I say, as if this revelation would alter everything – for me, for the Taj, for the Nalanda's plans and my publisher's. 'You have written about the Taj, sir?' 'Yes.' There's a small interval. 'I don't think they know, sir. They should definitely know.'

Nalanda is out of copies of *The Immortals*, says the attendant. He placed an order last month; there's been no movement. Either he's lying – or it's that balance of payment situation – or the distributor's acting up, a long path at the end of which my books lie in a warehouse. But is the distributor a person from Porlock – someone my mind's inventing? If there was no person from Porlock there would be a person from somewhere else, to make trouble, to come between the writer and their writing. Stevie Smith was right: we *need* our person from Porlock. A voice says: 'It's no one else. It's *you*. Figure it out.' In the meanwhile, as usual, I'm rebuffed. This is not a two-way street, I find. The Taj can be found in *The Immortals*, but *The Immortals* is not to be found in the Taj. I pick up a copy of *Time Out*. This is because I like guidebooks to cities I know.

Out of the bookshop, I'm in the lobby; walking towards the concierge, I turn right into the long corridor. They've closed off, for obvious reasons, side street and backstreet entrances that were, till 2008, open. A part of me regrets the sealing off. I wonder if – when the fear and the burden of responsibility this thing has generated have blown over – the doors will be opened again. Every restaurant in the corridor I pass, I make personal and historic notations for: 'This is the Harbour Bar; I was never fully aware of it till Shanbag of Strand Bookstall took my wife and me there in 1993, and we ate lobster chilli pepper'; 'Here's Golden Dragon (looks different now), where I first encountered chopsticks but never learned to use them. A few people were killed here.' And, also from the early eighties, this is where I first met Shobha De. It was soon after she'd become a De but before she appended the extra 'a' to her first name. She'd recently married someone who admired my father and lived in the same building as we did then – they took us out to dinner; or did my father take *them* out? The last time I came to Golden Dragon was in the nineties, during one of my post-marriage trips from Oxford, when my parents lived in Calcutta but we'd coincided in Bombay, and my father brought us here to rehearse past occasions though I don't think he could really afford the prices any more. The manager must have had a memory of him as the incredibly gentlemanly CEO of a big company (though long vanished from these parts) and, at the end of the dinner, charged him nothing. Remembering this, I hold in balance the same emotions I did from fifteen years ago: pleasure, that a man as striking and humane as my father should have been paid tribute to; pleasure, that even in a city as forgetful as this one, people can store away a memory of dignity; pleasure, that he should be acknowledged even when he'd gone from here and, on retirement, forfeited everything, as he'd forfeited his past upon Partition; guilt, that we'd always lived off the fat of the land. To those who have, more shall be given. If you have nothing, even the little you have is taken from you. This is unarguable. But the guilt is a spectre; it has no basis in reality. I wish it to be gone.

As usual, I stop at the photo display. I don't think I'm a celebrity watcher, but I've always found it arresting. They've returned, affirming continuity: of what was and will be. The attacks, for them, are just a blink of the eye. In fact, they've been through much more than the attacks. Bill Clinton, John Lennon, V.S. Naipaul, Nehru. Even Shobhaa De, larger than the rest, Cleopatra-like on a sankheda chair. *They* are the true survivors. They've known the fickleness of fortune, the travesty of renown – and are still with us. For some reason, I think I'll see Hitchcock among them. But Hitchcock never came to India, did he? Still, I forget a little later that he's *not* in the gallery. Which is the one bit of black and white in the corridor.

I press on. Two women of indeterminate nationality – they could be Latin American – walk towards and by me. They're followed by a middle-aged European in a sleeveless top and skirt. I'm in the foyer of the old wing now, and the swimming pool's on my right. Dusk's falling on the water. I think of Ramu. How, long ago, my parents and I had come here for dinner and, stepping out later, I'd gone quickly down the pavement (which is cordoned off now by barriers: no pedestrians) and, beneath one of the arches, on the steps of what used to be the chemist's, found Ramu. It was a year since I'd seen him. I hardly went to college any more, and (this was something I didn't know) neither did he. The year's gap was unremarkable. We were at that stage in our lives when friends were falling off. School friends are like relatives; you can't deny they were part of your growing up, but they come to mean nothing to you. That year, when I saw Ramu on the steps, a couple of our classmates had already gone to America. In the years to follow, others would leave – for Wharton, Carnegie Mellon, MIT. A bit like a wartime exodus. I said to Ramu, 'Hey, what's up? What're you doing here?' 'Nothing yaar,' fugitive in a way that was attractive. I presumed he was smoking marijuana. 'Don't ask.' 'My parents are a few steps behind me,' I said. 'Oh *shit*,' he said, and turned his face towards the arch. 'Rah-moo?' called my mother – she was glimmering in her sari and jewellery. 'How are you?' He stood up reluctantly. 'I'm okay Auntie.' 'Keeping yourself busy?' said my father.

Another time – I think it was 1986, when I rediscovered him in the months I spent in India between graduating from UCL and going back to Oxford – he said he could see himself working as one of the security personnel at the Taj. At this point, he'd been an addict for six or seven years, but was committed neither to being a full-blown goner nor to taking up normal life. 'Normal life' interested him in spurts, but then the enthusiasm for it seemed to vaguely die. The reasons for wanting a job as one of the Taj's security staff were, I think, manifold. First, he believed he looked the part. Also, the fact that, in security, you're doing something while you're not doing very much would have been integral to the job's appeal. Standing smartly, studying the middle distance. And he knew someone who had the job, and this planted the idea in his head. But he didn't know whom to approach or how to apply. The idea remained a possibility.

Before me is Gazdar. Full of the most delicately wrought jewellery. A curlicue of gold on a bangle; the miniature hive of an earring. I have neither the taste nor an eye for jewellery. But, a year ago, I came here to exchange my mother's mangalsutra (just as, now, I'm carrying her shoes). Its beads were like kalonji, or maybe fish roe. Why she wanted to give it up for something else after thirty years I had no idea: an old-age fit or whim. But she's in perfect possession of her senses and her whims have nothing to do with her years. The man at the counter – he was the one person in the shop – claimed he could remember her. I seemed to remember him, because he looked so familiar and appeared to belong firmly somewhere. I asked him if he was Mr Gazdar and he clarified he was a long-term employee – though he had the ease of a family member, of someone who'd been among the artefacts from a young age, and could regard them as both rarities and objects for trade. He had a slightly uxorious air – of a man who defers to other people's wives because he knows they call the shots. It's not as if Gazdar has hordes of customers, though. I can't afford its wares, but on the day of the mangalsutra exchange I saw a basrai pearl necklace (a fragile exoskeleton that made me nostalgic) which I thought I'd get my wife as an anniversary present.

How come Gazdar escaped ransacking in those three or four days? It doesn't make sense, somehow. I haven't had this conversation with the man who says he isn't Mr Gazdar. What he did tell me, though, is that he shut shop early that evening – or he'd have been in trouble.

Odd, I think. My mind's gone back to my mother's words. Her recounting of her Sylhet days were so vivid that it didn't occur to me that she was unhappy as a child. Even the privations she experienced while growing up had an aura of singularity in her accounts. Sometimes the tearful stories were amusing. Only once or twice did I get a sense of how hard it was. Evenly she'd said: 'I always knew that *that* wasn't going to be my life.' (By *that* she meant both Sylhet and the circumstances her family fell into after her father's death.) And indeed it wasn't. Much of her adult life was here in Bombay, part of it here, in the Taj. 'Your life will be one that you can't imagine now,' an astrologer had predicted. And it was clear, when she told me of the astrologer's words, that she *hadn't* imagined it. She was leading, by then, the life he'd foretold long ago. For me, foreknowledge was similar, but pointed in the opposite direction. This is why I feel a detachment and fraudulence as I walk to Joy Shoes. I knew *this* wouldn't be my life – Malabar Hill, Cuffe Parade, the Taj. 'The streets were never really mine.' I was going to be far away.

'The streets were never really mine.' In a way, this was true of my parents too. Of course, they owned their life in Malabar Hill, presided over it – I loved their benevolent reign. I myself never possessed my time here unequivocally. But when life in Bombay began to unravel after my father's retirement it was interesting how they made almost no attempt to not let it go. It was as if they were used to leaving. They'd left a few times before: on Partition; then to London; then from London. When it came to leaving, they knew how. Not that they were planning to depart from Bombay. But on some level they were preparing for departure. And, in acknowledgement, they began to let go of things. My mother anyway liked to give things away. It had been a startling habit from ever since I can remember, a tic. She'd gifted furniture to her music teacher, jewels and saris to relations. She even gave furniture to Ramu before we went away – to sell, ostensibly; but it was never sold, and came to adorn Ramu's room. Their last years here were marked by the sale of bits of my mother's jewellery. That's because my father's savings began to run out after retirement; his taxed income had been modest. Besides, he was financing my education in London; he'd borrowed money to buy the post-retirement flat. In 1986, between UCL and going to Oxford, I spent time with them in that small flat they'd moved to in Bandra. Then I got jaundice (though I'm careful to drink boiled water). I was transferred to Nanavati Hospital, to a 'deluxe' room in the old wing. It was terrible. At five in the morning, when I was woken up by a nurse who'd come to change the saline drip, I saw a large cockroach crawl across the floor. That afternoon, my parents moved me to a tip-top luxury room in the new wing of the Nanavati. How? My mother had sold a pair of diamond earrings. Both parents looked excited and vindicated. My father, at this point, saw at least some of my mother's jewellery as one might see bonds and debentures: as something meant to be encashed in need. I remember accompanying my parents on two trips into the stifling, entangled maze of Zaveri Bazaar when the bank balance had dipped again. I think it hurt my mother to lose some of those rings and pendants, and I've always wanted to give her back something, but never have. I've long wished to buy her those earrings. But the journeys to Zaveri Bazaar weren't desperate; they were full of anticipation. A thrilling climax. My parents, distracted and happy.

That idiot Ramu. He often stayed with us then, in those three years when we realised our time in Bombay was ending. I say 'idiot' with affection. Partly I say it because he seemed insensitive to the small upheaval that was occurring in our life. He was immersed in his own upheaval. But he's no idiot. I told him as much as we walked back and forth between the Gateway of India and the Radio Club, the sea black beside us. It was 1986; I was back from London and spending a year with my parents in the flat on St Cyril Road. We often discussed, that year, the possibility of selling the flat – our last pied-à-terre here. Every other day I'd take the local train to Churchgate to wander the streets in parts of the city where I'd grown up and gone to school, but where my parents no longer lived. It was on one of these sojourns that I ran into Ramu. He told me immediately of his addiction to brown sugar. 'I'm fucked,' he said. We renewed a friendship which, in school, had been neither slight nor thick, but convivial and fractious. He used to call me 'the poet' in school, both to heckle me and pay me a backhanded compliment – not because he'd read my poems but as a response to the fact that I didn't 'do' sports, wore glasses, was maladroit and kept my hair long. When we ran into each other again in 1986, there was no awkwardness between us. He made a presumption on my time which I immediately accepted. It was during a walk near the Taj that I said to him, 'But you're an intelligent man.' He studied me to check if I was mocking him. 'I know,' he said. 'I'm not stupid. But most stupid people are successful.' I nodded (I too was young). By 'intelligent', I meant the opposite of – a word hardly used these days – shallow. There was an intensity about his bewilderment, his rejection of normalcy; there always had been. Sometimes the rejection was opportunistic. His problem was boredom, and a sharp need to escape the things that bored him.

Our last days in Bombay were my happiest there – not, however, because I knew they were my last days. I had no idea. None of us did. But it was as if a premonition hung over us after the move to Bandra; the possibility of another – a final and unexpected – change. That came soon after my parents settled into the small new flat, the first property they owned in the city. Bandra was so different from everything we'd known. The churches; the remnants of a Goan idea of a neighbourhood; the low – sometimes derelict – cottages. It was as if my father had entered a period of banishment.

When I include myself in the business of leaving Bombay, I ignore the fact that I'd already left. I was in England at the time. In 1986, I took a year off in Bandra, but then went back to England. Yet mentally and emotionally I was with my parents, and in India. Inwardly, I accompanied and mimicked their shifts in location. The move to England meant less to me than the move to St Cyril Road.

Occasionally, I'd discover I was back in Oxford. But I barely noticed this. I was in Bandra. We were gearing up to leave.

Ramu, at the time, was drifting (as I was drifting between countries, pondering the future) in and out of addiction. He'd be clean for six months; then relapse. He'd say, on the phone, that he was 'absolutely fine'; two days later, he'd mutter he'd slipped. I began to feel wary when he said he was 'absolutely fine'. Because when he *was* okay, he merely sounded bored, already taking for granted the ennui of normal existence. The earnestness of 'absolutely fine' indicated that a transgression had taken place. Anyway, even to begin a conversation on the phone with 'How are you?' was to realise it was a loaded question; an interrogation, almost. But there was no way round ordinary courtesies.

No sooner had my parents moved to St Cyril Road than we began to weigh the option – playfully at first – of selling the apartment and moving to Calcutta. This was to ease my father's steadily growing debt. It wasn't difficult for us to have these discussions, because neither did we think they'd lead to an actual decision, and nor did we feel Bombay was really 'home'. I'd grown up here, but never belonged here. The fact that we were Bengalis prevented us from putting down roots in Bombay, and we underestimated our attachment to it. I say this because later we often missed it deeply. Still, I treasured each day in Bandra. That's because I was back home from Oxford, and every day in that small flat was important to me. I knew I'd have to go to Oxford again, and didn't want to. Bandra flowered around me. It felt familiar to me in a way that Malabar Hill and Cuffe Parade never had. I mean the stray dogs, the infinite afternoons, the low houses – our own flat was on the third storey, from which you could scrutinise the gulmohur blossoms that dominated the summer months at eye level. Every day in Bandra was precious – until I'd pack my bags again. Ramu would come to stay with me sometimes – for a day, or for two days, or even (wearing me out) for three. Our upheaval almost went unnoticed by us – so why should *he* have noticed?

Cloth bag in hand, I ascend the steps to the glass door. The handles to the doors unite in a horseshoe: the Joy Shoes logo. It's based on a breezy sketch executed by M.F. Husain. Those were the days! Inside, there's a picture Husain painted specially for the shop: one of his incandescent horses. Why an animal that flies off the earth when it runs should be an appropriate symbol for footwear is beyond me. Will these shoes make us fleet-footed? Are they to be hammered into our soles? There's a story here about the artist. Husain hardly wore footwear in those days. He went around the streets of Bombay barefoot. In school, we relished this anecdote, about Husain being refused entry into the Willingdon Club because he was shoeless. Hoity-toity rules: serves him right. Someone saw him hopping later on the hot macadam.

I enter and see the horse on my left. Husain must be in his nineties now. Ninety-three or -four. Of course, he doesn't live here any more. He's unofficially exiled. Still, why not let the horse hang where it always did? A Husain is a Husain.

'Hello, sir?' says – but his name's gone from my head. 'Exchange, no?' He smiles and adds: 'When you came back?'

'Just earlier today.'

He shakes his head mildly: not so much a yes as acceptance.

'Mummy okay?'

'She's all right, actually.' In Bombay, you subtly shift your speech so you sound like the one speaking to you. You don't want to stand out. You want to sound more or less like you did when you were twelve: nothing's changed.

'She called,' he says, half smiling.

A woman in a pistachio sari, whose white foot cranes over a shoe, lifts her head. She looks candidly at me. It's a look that one well-to-do person passes prematurely to another.

'Really?'

'Just now only. She was asking if you came. She gave instructions for her shoes and your wife's shoes.'

The woman in the sari looks vindicated; perhaps the shoe fits.

There are mirrors everywhere for us to examine our feet.

I step out discreetly to get a better signal. Not far from me is the palatial back entrance of the hotel, locked with finality.

'Which colour do you want?' I ask my wife.

'Tell them to bring out the priya,' she advises. She vacillates: 'See what the beige looks like. Also the black. No, actually I have a black one. Check the white. Why don't you decide for yourself? Actually, don't.'

She blames my mother for her reliance on Joy Shoes – they were unknown to her before she got married. Now she wears little else. By the time we met in Oxford, Bombay was history for me: very recent history, but decidedly the past. I revealed my life in it to her piecemeal, guiltily, with a sly boastfulness, conveying, without much effort, how literally incredible it was and also how easily I let it go when I had the chance.

I walk back in. The colours of the classic designs are black, white, gold and beige. But I've also spotted magenta on the heels. My mother is loyal to the priya. She's incapable of wearing heels; she has a broken foot. My wife, too, abhors heels and the glitzier options. (I pick up a glass slipper and wonder if I can tempt her.) The classic designs don't evolve hugely. I've noted them for decades: they become distilled. Extraneous bits – which you realise are extraneous after they're gone – are constantly sacrificed; the shoes grow sleeker and sparser.

Munna has appeared. Holding forth into the receiver, behind the till. Busy, but reassuring. I recall he's a Muslim. But why can't I escape this thought? Distracted, he waves. The bonds of mutual loyalty are strong. Is he a Vohra? There are many of them in Bombay; they're prosperous.

'Hello, hello, hello,' he says, in a tone of congratulatory disbelief. 'How are *you*?'

'Haven't seen you in a while,' I concede, patting his shoulder. 'I came here about a year ago for a very short trip' – he nods – 'when my new book came out, but I couldn't come to the shop.'

'But your wife came to take some priya, no?' he asks, his memory razor-sharp. Narrowing his eyes, he says, 'She's not here this time?'

I shake my head. 'No, but she made it a point to send me.'

'That's good, that's good,' he says melodiously, smiles, scratches his beard. 'What's the name of the new book? I'm sure I read about it in the evening papers – or maybe in the *Times*.'

'*The Immortals*.'

'That's it!' he exclaims, glancing at a stub half submerged in the card machine. The roll's stuck. 'What's it about?' This is a version of the 'How are you?' he's put to me already.

I think of a succinct way of holding his attention. 'You know, I've described Joy Shoes in it.'

'No!' Agog, but the steely bit of his attention is still fixed on the stub.

'There's a young man in the novel,' I continue, 'comes from an affluent family, but pretends to be poor – wears torn kurtas, frayed jeans, but' – I smile into his eyes – 'he's always in Joy Shoes sandals.'

'Ha!' he cries, wondering what these behavioural traits add up to. 'What is it? It's a novel? Where can I find it?'

Good question, I think, and claim insouciantly, 'Just check in the bookshops.'

No one is sure any more what the novel is. The word has unprecedented currency.

He shakes the roll loose. 'Must get a copy!'

My reason for telling Munna about Joy Shoes in *The Immortals* is not only to elicit a response, or to make him feel like an honour's been bestowed on him. For me (given that my writing is accused of coming directly from life), the aftermath of the book, in which people believe they've been written about and start to find their own correspondences, is the most interesting chapter.

'But glad to see all's well! Terrible stuff, what happened.' I've been to Bombay once since November 2008, but feel like I haven't. 'I was watching it on TV in England. Turned on the news. I couldn't believe my eyes.'

'My God!' says Munna, losing his smile. 'We had to go to a wedding that night, so we left early. Usually we begin shutting at eight.' He gestures to his right without moving his eyes. 'Some of those fellows came in from there.'

He focuses.

'Mom's sandals are ready, no?'

'I think he's gone in to check.'

We glance at the room, small as a monk's cell, in which shoes are secreted.

Passing along the hotel corridor, I turn right and come to the majestic red-carpeted staircase. I climb up the stairs; each step is capacious, as if people ascending were expected to make giant strides sideways. There's a lift, but no one in their right mind would enter the shell of the lift when the staircase is available.

On the top of the stairs, on the left, is what for me is the main, the old, entrance to the Sea Lounge; but this, of course, is closed. Reaching the first floor, the entrance is on the right, diagonally. The Sea Lounge has had to be restored from scratch; it was reopened recently. Once I'm in, I find things have a rehearsed air: the notes on the piano of 'Yesterday Once More'; the spacious sofas inhabited by large groups along the sides and in the centre. I want a table by the window, where only couples sit. There they are, presenting their profiles, painterly against the light. They're deep in themselves. There's a free table by the middle window.

A tall waiter in white shirt and trousers and brown apron escorts me to the table and silently takes my order of Darjeeling tea and a plate of cookies. I don't like Darjeeling tea, but I'm buying time. It's not that far from dinner. Besides, I don't want to spend five hundred rupees on bhel puri. I notice the waiters' uniforms haven't changed. But almost all the waiters are new. In the seventies, the Sea Lounge had a regularity in my consciousness, as my parents used to come here late Saturday morning and occupy one of these tables by the window. Their order, like other things about them at the time, was unvarying: chilli cheese toast, tea. The Sea Lounge had a menu of arcane bites: chicken or mushroom vol-au-vents, the cream stored beneath volcanic flaps; Scandinavian open sandwiches (the idea of an 'open sandwich', where the filling was left exposed, unprotected, was boldly counter-intuitive). Then there were bhel and sev puri, served on pristine china. My mother insisted we couldn't eat these off the street for fear of jaundice; but in the Sea Lounge, where they were made in conditions of uncompromising hygiene, her love of bhel was very evident. Sitting at the table, I glance out of the window on my right, while the pianist tinkles away and I follow the notes, reconstituting the words: *Those were such happy times and not so long ago ... Every sha-la-la-la ... still shines ...*

I get up. I know the toilets are far away, and a tour awaits through long corridors. I temporarily abandon the table, leaving the Joy Shoes bag on a chair.

Before stepping out, I eavesdrop on the pianist. A deeply serious man. Reticent, he glances at me, then returns to what looks – even sounds – like a bit of typing. The notes are clunky.

I go through the doors, turn left; this stretch is like a balcony in a theatre. Soon I'm at the inner corridor, where I turn left again; on my right is the Crystal Room – I might have been tempted to wander towards it and peep in, except I know that it's still under construction. Much at this end of the first floor has been gutted. That great and useless space must have once, before I was born, been used for celebrations and felicitations, but I only remember its Christmas lunches, weddings and sari exhibitions. I move away from it. It's a long walk down the corridor to the toilets.

When you come to the end, you feel not so much that you're in another part of the hotel as in a different city. I chance upon an ornate and dishevelled scene. Two handsome liveried men – employees of the hotel – stand watching a band of noisy people in bright clothes: bandhani saris; turbans. Maybe they're wedding guests (poor relations), or the family of musicians or artistes who've come to perform at one of the restaurants. In which dialect are they shouting to each other? I go into the toilet and a wave of perfectly maintained features – stonework framing basins; antique fittings on taps – engulfs me. I empty my bladder thoroughly. When I emerge, most of the party outside have disbanded – it was only for a moment they'd come together here. A liveried man is fading into the distance.

Quiet has re-established itself with their departure. This is where the rooms are. Quiet, quiet. Beyond the access of interlopers. Those men made for this wing, of course, and the cat-and-mouse game lasted four days. People fleeing, hiding, dying, changing location at strange hours, led by staff.

The CCTV footage captures flashes of it: the men with guns, intent; the guests and staff transiting at odd times of the night. All of them trapped, circling this wing. It's in the bad lighting of the CCTV video that the hotel echoes the mausoleum it's named after – in which tourists arc round the tombs encased in marble, shrouded in the perpetual semi-dark of mourning, where they can't take pictures. As a result, there's no record of our visits to Mumtaz Mahal and Shah Jahan's resting places. The CCTV footage too, when you see it, seems almost an impossibility.

How long will it take for the Crystal Room to be put together? They must be working on it at this very moment, although, as I turn right, I hear no sound; no hammering, no drilling. I'm back in the Sea Lounge. They've done a good job. It's not so much a twin of the room that was destroyed, or a replacement. What they have tried to do is follow the example of the moving image of the disintegrating object or edifice played backwards, so that the shards and fragments, as you keep watching, fly up instantaneously and regain their old places until completion is achieved and, at last, there's no discontinuity between past and present. Accustomed as we are to technology, we know it's an illusion – the shards are all there somewhere; it's just that the film has been reversed. Is this why Benjamin saw in Klee's *Angelus Novus* (which 'shows an angel looking as though he is about to move away from something he is fixedly contemplating') the 'angel of history'? 'His face is turned toward the past,' he says. 'Where we perceive a chain of events, he sees one single catastrophe which keeps piling wreckage upon wreckage and hurls it in front of his feet. The angel would like to stay, awaken the dead, and make whole what has been smashed. But a storm is blowing from Paradise; it has got caught in his wings with such violence that the angel can no longer close them. This storm irresistibly propels him into the future to which his back is turned, while the pile of debris before him grows skyward.' To be in the Taj is to experience its emergence from this storm. Like the angel, it has turned its back to the future it's once more moving towards. When I look around me in the Sea Lounge, I see its composure and reinstatement – the improvements are so unobtrusive you don't notice them – but I'm also confronting the debris.

'Should I pour the tea, sir?'
But he *will* pour it. There's a rigour to his posture; he stays very straight while the tea trickles out. Three lightly tanned cookies on the plate. I bite one. It turns to powder.

This would have been a good moment to call Ramu. I look out of the window. He lives not far away. It's not like Ramu to consent to a regime that's made him incommunicado; but maybe there was no other remedy. Ordinarily, I might not feel the need to chat; but the fact that I have no choice except not to is making me restless. Anyway, our conversations are silly; they're designed to return us to our schoolboy personae. It's as if we haven't moved on from those days when we're with each other. I always hated school. Ramu both loved and hated it. All his best years were there, he claims. Yet he hated its glamorising of sport – not because (like me) he was bad at sport, but because he was so good at it. His housemasters wanted to exploit his abilities – he resisted, to their dismay. They never forgave him. Besides, the school was meant for rich children. Why did his father (he'd asked me), an ordinary middle-class man with a small business, put him in a school meant for the Tatas, the Dubashes, the Ginwallas, the sons and daughters of CEOs, government ministers and film actresses? Ramu's adept at apportioning blame.

I gesture to a man who's standing in my line of vision, by the old exit.

'Bill please.'

'Yes, sir.'

Before he recedes, I say: 'The Sea Lounge looks good.'

He nods, indulgent.

'But the staff seem new,' I confide.

'Yes, sir,' he agrees, prolonging his puzzled nod. 'Mostly new only.'

'Where's the old staff?'

'Some left.' He hesitates. 'Some died.'

'Died?'

'Yes, sir.' He studies me; pauses, apologetic.

'I see . . .' I fall silent. 'So that's why – But *you've* worked here for a long time. I've seen you before.'

'Thirty years.' He explains: 'I was not here that day.'

When I'm leaving, he's standing by the macaroons.

'Sir,' he says.

I stop.

'I too feel I've seen you before.'

I nod but say nothing. The pianist's at it.

He continues shyly: 'Are you in the High Court?'

I shake my head. Then add: 'My father used to come here a lot many years ago.'

He appears pained, groping – till something alters. His eyes widening, he asks: 'Mr Chaudhuri?'

I'm disbelieving, as if I've glimpsed a ghost. These are the last vestiges of our life here.

'Yes. He's my father.'

'Very good people,' he says, unexpected with this belated certificate. 'Sir and madam.' ■

It seems to me that all writing is travel writing. All writing is an act of colonisation and of exoticising. There are no correct procedures. Writing is by its very nature an intrusion: voyeuristic; fetishistic; impolite; self-serving – the self is the finished piece of writing. Its effects may be much more noble, but not necessarily. We know that writers, like readers, perform their acts of transportation regardless of any physical distances they may travel: Emily Dickinson; Joseph Cornell (their open cages). If you laugh and tell me I am only speaking metaphorically, I will reply: what other way do you expect me to speak? Metaphor is Greek for 'transfer'. A poet told me this. Writing is being a tourist on your own street; writing is spying on your neighbour; writing is having five addresses; four names; three passports; two faces; one small indivisible identity – that does, however, get split. Bedroom window. Hotel window. Either way, nostalgia is Greek for 'return home'. And that is the bedrock of all writing. A stranger told me this. ∎

CONTRIBUTORS

William Atkins is the author of *The Moor*. His book about the world's deserts will be published in 2018.

Tara Bergin was born in Dublin. Her first collection of poems, *This is Yarrow*, was awarded the 2014 Seamus Heaney Centre for Poetry Prize and the 2014 Shine/Strong Award for best first collection by an Irish author. She currently lives in the north of England.

Emily Berry's debut book of poems, *Dear Boy*, won the 2013 Forward Prize for Best First Collection and the 2014 Hawthornden Prize. Her second collection, *Stranger, Baby*, is published by Faber & Faber.

Amit Chaudhuri's latest novel is *Odysseus Abroad*. He is also a musician and essayist. His new novel, *Friend of My Youth*, is forthcoming from Faber & Faber in the UK and Penguin Random House in India.

Rana Dasgupta is a British novelist and essayist. His novel *Solo* won the 2010 Commonwealth Writers' Prize. His latest book, *Capital*, is a documentary portrait of New Delhi in the recent era of economic growth, poverty and corruption. He is a visiting lecturer at Brown University.

Geoff Dyer's books include *Jeff in Venice*, *Otherwise Known as the Human Condition* and, most recently, *White Sands: Experiences from the Outside World*. He lives in California.

David Flusfeder's most recent novel is *John the Pupil*. He teaches at the University of Kent.

Janine di Giovanni is the Middle East editor of *Newsweek*. A war and conflict reporter for over twenty-five years, she is a member of the Council on Foreign Relations and was recently made an Ochberg Fellow at Columbia University for her work on trauma victims. Her most recent book is *The Morning They Came for Us: Dispatches From Syria*. She was awarded the 2016 Courage in Journalism Award.

Eliza Griswold is a poet and journalist. She is currently a Berggruen Fellow at Harvard Divinity School.

Xiaolu Guo is a writer and film-maker. Her novels include *A Concise Chinese–English Dictionary for Lovers*, shortlisted for the 2007 Orange Prize for Fiction, *UFO in Her Eyes* and *I Am China*, longlisted for the 2015 Baileys Women's Prize for Fiction. Her memoir *Once Upon a Time in the East* is published in 2017. She was one of *Granta*'s Best of Young British Novelists in 2013. She lives in Berlin and London.

Mohsin Hamid is the author of three novels, including *The Reluctant Fundamentalist*. His latest novel, *Exit West*, is forthcoming from Hamish Hamilton in the UK and Riverhead in the US. He lives in Lahore.

Lindsey Hilsum is the international editor of Britain's *Channel 4 News* and the author of *Sandstorm: Libya in the Time of Revolution*. She is currently working on a biography of the late war correspondent, Marie Colvin.

Pico Iyer's most recent books include *The Art of Stillness* and *The Man Within My Head*.

Ian Jack edited *Granta* between 1995 and 2007, and now writes for the *Guardian*.

Justin Jin shoots epic photographic narratives about social change for the world's best publications. His last project, *Zone of Absolute Discomfort*, was published in *Granta* 125: After the War. His website is www.justinjin.com.

Carl De Keyzer's work has been exhibited internationally in venues such as the Canon Image Center in Amsterdam and the San Francisco Art Institute.

Lu Nan translates from the Chinese. She is an editor at People's Literature Publishing House in China, promoting Chinese literature abroad.

Zeyar Lynn is a Rangoon-based poet, critic, writer and translator. He has instigated a wider appreciation of postmodern and L=A=N=G=U=A=G=E poetry forms in Burma. His collections include *Distinguishing Features* and *Kilimanjaro*.

Andrew McConnell is an Irish photographer. He has covered the conflict in the Democratic Republic of Congo, life under Robert Mugabe, electronic waste in Ghana and the ongoing occupation of Western Sahara. He is represented by Panos Pictures.

Robert Macfarlane's books include *Mountains of the Mind*, *The Wild Places*, *The Old Ways* and, most recently, *Landmarks*, which was shortlisted for the 2015 Samuel Johnson Prize. He is a Fellow of Emmanuel College, Cambridge.

Adam Marek is the author of two short-story collections, *Instruction Manual for Swallowing* and *The Stone Thrower*. His work has appeared on Radio 4 and in many anthologies, including *The Penguin Book of the British Short Story*.

Hoa Nguyen was born in the Mekong Delta and raised in the Washington DC area. Her poetry collections include *As Long As Trees Last*, *Red Juice* and *Violet Energy Ingots*. She lives in Toronto.

Edna O'Brien has written over twenty works of fiction, along with biographies of James Joyce and Lord Byron. She is the recipient of many awards, including the Irish PEN Lifetime Achievement Award and the Ulysses Medal. She is an honorary member of the American Academy of Arts and Letters. Her most recent novel is *The Little Red Chairs*.

Xan Rice is features editor of the *New Statesman*. His last piece for *Granta* was 'The Aviators', in issue 101.

Safiya Sinclair's first collection, *Cannibal*, won the 2015 *Prairie Schooner* Book Prize in Poetry and a 2016 Whiting Award. Her poems have appeared in *Poetry*, the *Kenyon Review*, the *Nation* and elsewhere. She is currently a PhD candidate in literature and creative writing at the University of Southern California.

Samanth Subramanian is a Dublin-based writer. His most recent book, *This Divided Island: Stories from the Sri Lankan War*, was shortlisted for the 2015 Samuel Johnson Prize. His writing has appeared in the *New Yorker*, the *New York Times* and the *Guardian*, among other publications.

Colin Thubron is a writer and novelist, who has written primarily on Central Asia, Russia and China. His books include *Among the Russians*, *Behind the Wall*, *In Siberia* and *Shadow of the Silk Road*. In 2010 he became President of the Royal Society of Literature.

Alexis Wright is a member of the Waanyi nation of the Gulf of Carpentaria, and is the author of *The Swan Book*, *Carpentaria* and *Grog War*.

A Yi's books include the novel *A Perfect Crime* and the collections *Grey Stories* and *The Bird Saw Me*. His work has appeared in the *Guardian* and *Paper Republic*. He is the editor-in-chief of the literary magazine *Chutzpah*. He lives in Beijing.